5/92

D0591048

To Lord Crickhowell
Chairman of the NRA
Board, with greetings
and good wishes from
the Chairman of the
Broads Authority.

July '94

£5

M

1914

Wetlands

David Bellamy and Brendan Quayle

W E T L A N D S

AN EXPLORATION OF THE LOST WILDERNESS
OF EAST ANGLIA

Research by Deborah Bartlett MA (CANTAB)

Photographs by John Beatty
and Richard Denyer

SIDGWICK & JACKSON
LONDON

For Michael

The authors would like to give special thanks to Mark Eckstein, Jonathan
Wallace, Rita Brownsword and Michelle Turnbull of David Bellamy Associates;
Aitken Clarke and Diana Shipp of the Norfolk Broads Authority; Jeremy
Bryant; Peter Bower and Barney Matthews of Wherry Yacht Charter, Wroxham;
and Ingrid, Hilary and Carey of Sidgwick & Jackson.

First published in Great Britain in 1990 by Sidgwick & Jackson Limited

ISBN 0-283-99983-7

Typeset by Rowland Phototypesetting Limited,
Bury St Edmunds, Suffolk

Printed by Butler & Tanner Limited, Frome, Somerset
for Sidgwick & Jackson Limited
1 Tavistock Chambers, Bloomsbury Way
London WC1A 2SG

Frontispiece: The wind in the reeds at Burgh Castle Reach.

Contents

Preface

'Dick and Dorothea Collum had never been to Norfolk before.' So starts Arthur Ransome's children's classic *Coot Club*, a book which introduced so many people to the Norfolk Broads, to the pleasure of boating and to an encounter with the very best of England's last remaining wetland wilderness.

When Ransome was writing, that wilderness was in better fettle than it is now, but even then it was in poor shape compared to what it once was, in the last century and the centuries before. For the Norfolk Broads is all that remains of a much larger wetland and fenland area which took in much of Norfolk and Suffolk and nearly all of Cambridgeshire and beyond to the west, north and south. But all that has been lost in time, mostly due to the actions of man. Ransome's Broads, together with the odd bit of fen here and there, are a mere remnant of a glorious biological past, England's lost wetland wilderness.

However, we have to count some blessings. The fact that we have the Broads, and the fact that we ever had the rest of those wetlands at all is due to an accident of ecological history. Our remaining wetlands are indeed a once upon a time, story tale world, a land that never should have been,

for they are in reality the domain of the sea.

As the Earth's ever-present greenhouse, the atmosphere, brought the last Ice Age into temperate and temporary meltdown, saltwater refilled the basin of the North Sea, overflooding the horseshoe of flatland which flanks the Wash. What King Canute failed to do, the growth of common plants like grass and sedge easily accomplished, and on a massive scale. The processes of natural succession held back the tides slowly, creating a sweet water wonderland of marsh, swamp and fen, overflowing with plants, wildfowl, fish and birds.

But after all that, the fact that we still have any of those wetlands left to boast about at all, is down to a series of further 'Ifs':

If nature had been left entirely to her own devices, the sea defences would have been breached again and again. But generations of engineers worked with the earth and wind to keep the salt at bay, or at least out in the Wash.

If the natural processes of succession had gone to their terminal end, great tracts of the wetland would have been replaced by broadleaf woodland. But generations of marshpeople made their homes of wattle and daub thatched with reed and fed and bedded their animals on products of the marsh and fen so keeping the wetlands open.

If the East Anglian winters hadn't been so cold then perhaps the medieval pit diggers would never have created that wild, wet, watery wonderland of lakes and shallows: the Broads. But they were and they did, and so today we have a multi-billion pound tourist resource.

If coal hadn't been in use by the time the Little Ice Age turned much of the area into a skaters' paradise, they might have dug some more. Just think what could have been accomplished with modern equipment!

If Peter Scott, budding skating champion, Olympic yachtsman and eventual father of wildlife conservation hadn't visited the area in his youth, perhaps the Wildfowl Trust and the World Wide Fund for Nature would have been longer in the making.

If generations of natural historians hadn't had the same opportunity to visit the remnants of this wet wilderness then the Royal Society of Nature Conservation and the Ramsar Wetlands Convention might never have got off the ground or onto the statute books and there might never have been a Broadlands National Park.

That's an awful lot of 'ifs'. All the more reason perhaps to read this book with care and then, with equal care, leaving only a gentle stern wake and taking only pictures and local produce, go and see it for yourself.

Savour, 'great clouds along pacific skies', the 'thrilling sweet and rotten river smell' the pull of a tiller in your hand, the boom of bittern, the sweet song of skylarks. Discover the wet wilderness, lost amongst ordered fields and urban sprawl, a reed fringed *terra incognita* waiting for your own personal voyage of discovery, a passageway from all our pasts, to all our futures, if only we care enough.

David Bellamy

In Search of the Lost Wilderness

Wetlands Lost and Found

When you work with water, you have to know and respect it.
When you labour to subdue it, you have to understand that one day
it may rise up and turn all your labours to nothing.

GRAHAM SWIFT, *Waterland*

Once upon a time in the east, there was a vast wind-blown wilderness of marsh and mud, filled with wild flowers, fishes and wetland animals. The air was thick with the cries of water-birds. On the ground, the flats, salt marshes, fen edges and riverbanks were awash with countless thousands of wading birds, multi-coloured and on stilt-like legs, and people were few and far between. East Anglia was a no-man's land, where wind and water reigned supreme, a wild wetness stretching to infinity.

That was the time after the Ice Age, when the sea was in charge of the fortunes of the land. But that time was not to last. More and more men and women began to appear on the landscape, on the dry bits between the salt flats and the wader pools, on the fens and the water-edge. They brought new technologies and ideas, new ways of living on the land, and new ways of taming the unruly waters of East Anglia to suit their uses.

But even when more densely populated, this great wet wilderness yielded up its independence most reluctantly. It remained a foreboding place, where cold winds from the North Sea blew across the land, eating into the marrow of every living thing, creeping into every nook and corner, bending reeds and sweeping ripples across the silent inland waterways. The wetland folk were a reserved lot, a race apart, feared by inland peoples for their marsh magic and their wild ways.

The ecology of the land was rich; a myriad of diverse plants and insects flourished and multiplied. Food was bountiful in the form of fish, eels, game and wild birds. The living for people was good on the whole, but life itself was short, for there was disease too, in particular the ague. But that was when the lives of women and men were like those of the

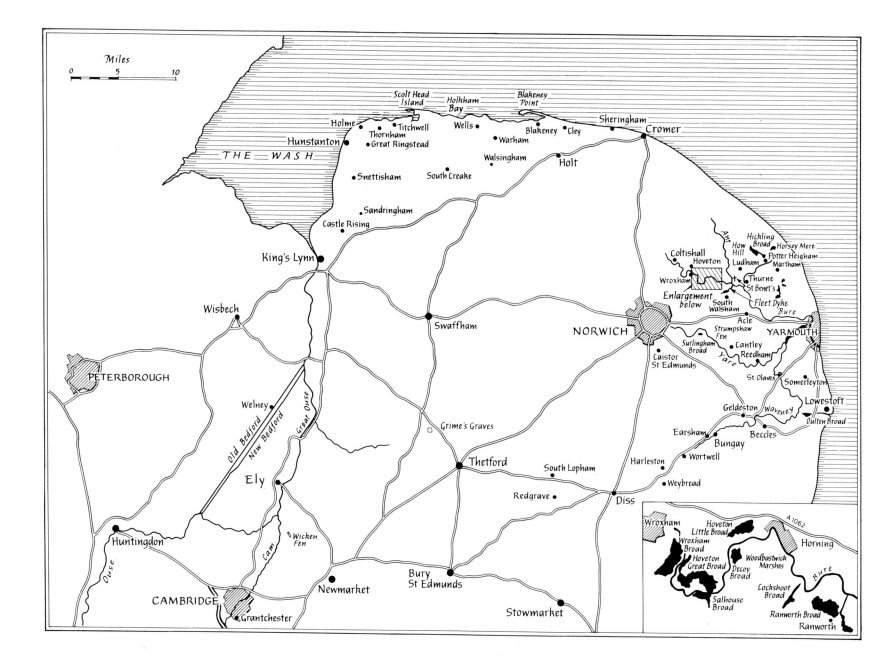

Miles
0   5   10

Scolt Head
Island   Holkham
Bay   Blakeney
Point

Holme   Titchwell   Wells   Blakeney Cley   Sheringham   Cromer
Thornham   Warham
Hunstanton   Great Ringstead   Holt

THE WASH   Walsingham

Snettisham   South Creake

Sandringham

Castle Rising   Coltishall   Hickling Horsey Mere
                                                                                    Hoveton Broad
                                                                            How   Ludham   Potter Heigham
King's Lynn   Hill   Martham
                                                                         Wroxham   Thurne
                                                                                        St Benet's
                                                                         Enlargement
                                                                         below   South   Fleet Dyke
                                                                                     Walsham   Bure

Wisbech   Swaffham   NORWICH   Acle
                                                                    Strumpshaw   YARMOUTH
                                                                    Fen
                                                              Surlingham   Cantley
                                                              Broad   Reedham
PETERBOROUGH   Caistor
                                                         St Edmunds   St Olaves
                                                                                   Somerleyton

                                                                                        Lowestoft
Welney   Geldeston Waveney
                                          Grime's Graves   Oulten Broad

Old Bedford   Earsham   Beccles
New Bedford   Bungay
Great Ouse   Harleston   Wortwell
                                    Thetford
                          Ely   South Lopham   Weybread
                    Cam   Diss
                              Wicken   Redgrave
                              Fen

Huntingdon
Ouse

                              Newmarket   Bury
CAMBRIDGE   St Edmunds
        Grantchester   Stowmarket

Wroxham   Hoveton   A 1062
                 Little Broad
        Wroxham   Horning
        Broad   Hoveton   Woodbastwick
                 Great Broad Marshes
                          Decoy
                          Broad   Cockshoot   Bure
                 Salhouse   Broad
                 Broad
                                    Ranworth Broad
                                    Ranworth

East Anglia (opposite). Map by Neil Hyslop.

Masters of wind, past and present: Halvergate (below).

animals and the plants, part of the great unwritten plan, the law of the wild.

But times changed and humankind got the upper hand. They drained the wet wilderness. They dug ditches and raised dykes to hold back the flood, they built sluices and wind-pumps to reduce its swelling might, and they redirected what was left of the water into man-made channels along the sides of the land. Nature retreated to the fen edge and to new pits dug by men, or held fast to the river corridors that remained, to the Ouse and the Nene and the Cam, the Bure and the Waveney.

In time, the dry peat-lands on the Fens sank, forming acres upon acres of agricultural land, rich in the nutrients of sea silt and land peat. And there were other benefits too. The ague or malaria, which had cursed the human occupation of the wetlands, carried from body to body by the spotted mosquito, was cast out along with the waters. The mosquito lost his habitat, the wild wet endless marsh. And with this little winged monster there went the excuse for yet another curse upon the local population, their dependence upon opium. This was used initially to alleviate the symptoms of the ague but eventually as a stimulant in itself, like the reedy exotic cannabis, which once grew in profusion along the marsh edge. As for the people:

They ceased to be water people and became land people; they ceased to be fish and fowl and became plumbers of the land. They joined in the destiny of the Fens, which was to strive not for but against water. . . . Or perhaps they did not cease to be water people. Perhaps they became amphibians. Because if you drain land you are intimately concerned with water; you have to know its ways. Perhaps at heart they always knew, in spite of their land preserving efforts, that they belonged to the old, prehistoric flood.

GRAHAM SWIFT, *Waterland*

The water, the ague and the dope may have gone. But a landscape formed by water, and lying between greedy stretches of it, left man with the everpresent problem of keeping the water under control. For East Anglia does flood; the sea and the inland waters do swell and rise. If the pundits of the Greenhouse Effect are right and sea levels throughout the world do rise, a time of water will come again – sooner rather than later.

Not Just a Wet Blanket

The traditional view of wetlands as wastelands is not peculiar to East Anglia; it has pervaded the thinking of civilizations around the world. Reclaim the land from water for agriculture, for building; drain for a better and safer future; these were rallying cries well before Vermuyden's early drainage schemes first began to tame the dank mysterious Fens of the seventeenth century.

Draining wetlands has a commercial and an agricultural logic. Wetlands are amongst the most fertile ecosystems in the world, producing up to eight times as much plant matter as an average field of wheat. With the rich topsoils that result from a vigorous drainage programme, wetlands have provided the breadbaskets that fed and fired the great civilizations. The wetlands and deltas of the Euphrates, the Tigris, the Nile and the Mekong succoured the early civilizations that shaped the history of mankind.

And who would deny the culture of the marshes where water has been controlled, a culture of boats and barges, of mighty horses and stone windmills? Who would take away the skills of the basket-maker and the thatcher, the fisherman and others whose craft and livelihood has depended upon the wetlands?

But the wetlands of the world are fragile environments, too easily damaged by pollution, over-zealous drainage schemes and population pressure. Popular images of marshes, swamps, fens and mires do not endear them to the public: 'What do we want that for? Drain it, plough it, tame it, dry it, take away the uncertainty, the vapours and the smells.' In the public mind, wetlands have for centuries remained the preserve of fugitives and ne'er-do-wells who have lurked in the misty backwaters. Even the definitions applied to wetland habitats are shrouded in confusion: what are the differences between a mire and a swamp? Or a fen and a bog? Most people don't know, or care.

But the differences between a marsh and a swamp mean a great deal to the plants and animals that live there. It is this rich mosaic of habitats – from open water, through reed-bed, fen, marsh and bog – that maintains both the productivity and the diversity of wetlands, a diversity as essential to man as it is to nature.

Of course, the role and importance of wetland has always been apparent to those who make a living out of them. In East Anglia as elsewhere, wildfowling, fishing, thatching and a host of other traditional industries have supported people for centuries. But it is the indirect benefits that have remained largely unnoticed, despite the fact that they have a more important and far-reaching impact.

Wetlands perform vital roles in controlling and dissipating the flow of water, reducing the effects of flooding and storm surges. They act as giant filters, removing sediments, pollutants and fertilizers that might otherwise enter rivers and affect navigation, fisheries and even our health and well-being. Productive grazed marshlands provide prime agricultural

But where's the catch? Salhouse Broad (opposite).

Down amongst the wet meadow grasses: Strumpshaw Fen (right).

pastureland for sheep and cattle. Today's wetlands, particularly places like the East Anglian Broads, are also an exciting recreational resource for boaters, anglers and birdwatchers, for people who take pleasure from the wind, the water and the creatures of earth and air.

The Wet Foot Brigade

The range of habitats that make up a wetland is reflected in the diversity of plants and animals that make their homes in this watery world. The plethora of habitats has encouraged wildlife to specialize, and specialization often leads to rarity. For example, the caterpillars of the swallowtail butterfly dine mainly on milk parsley, and the increasing rarity of this plant has had its effect on the distribution of Britain's largest and most flamboyant butterfly.

Similarly, the water soldier, a shy, retiring water plant that spends much of its year submerged in slow-flowing ditches, only coming to the surface to flower and set seed, has suffered as a result of drainage and water pollution. Water spiders, dragonflies, moths, birds and mammals have all suffered as the pace of change increases throughout the marshland world.

Their very rareness encourages extra human interest. For botanists, birdwatchers and a plethora of boffins, the Norfolk and Suffolk Broads and what is left of the Fens are a mecca in certain seasons. They come to hear the boom of the bittern across the marsh; they come to see rare plants like the marsh sow thistle and the fen orchid. They come to see the rare native otter, now being bred for re-introduction to replace those that are lost.

However, it is the characteristic mix of wetland plant and animal communities that provides the real interest for naturalists in the Anglian wetlands – the intricate relationships of common and not so common, that have helped to create one of the jewels of our natural heritage. Man too has played a part in this matrix. Over the centuries, grazing and management practices have helped to create a stable and predictable regime suitable for many plants.

The botanical diversity of grazed marshland can be quite extraordinary, provided that traditional techniques and acceptable levels of livestock are maintained. However, as the pace of agricultural change quickens, this delicate balance is disturbed. Regular application of fertilizers, re-seeding, draining and a host of other improvements do not suit the interests of many plants and animals. What is left of the wet wilderness is being tamed, but at what cost?

From a purely monetary point of view, it makes sense to improve food yields per former wetland acre. But when other factors are introduced, such as the quality of life, protection of wildlife, water quality and flood protection value, it becomes more tricky to balance the books.

What value could be put on a landscape once lost, particularly one as distinctive as that of East Anglia? For one thing, it is exceedingly flat.

From the raised banks of the leam, it stretched away to the horizon, its uniform colour, peat-black, varied only by the crops that grew upon it – grey-green potato leaves, blue-green beet leaves, yellow-green wheat: its uniform levelness broken only by the furrowed and dead-straight lines of ditches and drains, which, depending on the state of the sky and the angle of the sun, ran like silver, copper or golden wires across the fields and which, when you stood and looked at them, made you shut one eye and fall prey to fruitless meditations on the laws of perspective.

GRAHAM SWIFT, *Waterland*

Talking of perspective, if you cast your eye towards the horizon and raise your neck just a little bit, you are staring straight at another feature of the landscape of East Anglia which seems to deny the normal laws of perspective: the sky. It is somehow huger here, bigger and grander and more dominant than any sky that you might encounter anywhere else. Because the land is so flat, your breadth of view embraces an almost perfect hemisphere. You can watch uninterruptedly all the transforming colours, shapes and motions of the day, while at night the sky is awash with star cluster upon star cluster. This landscape of sky has been noted by many poets and writers.

Overhead the arch of Heaven spread more ample than elsewhere, as over the open sea; and that vastness gave, and still gives such cloudlands, such sunrises, such sunsets, as can be seen nowhere else within these isles.

CHARLES KINGSLEY, *Hereward the Wake*

Perhaps this flatness of land and this dominance of sky gives the lie to the whole lost wetlands saga: that the landscapes of East Anglia owe more to the sea than they do to the land. The first loss was the sea's. But that loss is, aesthetically at least, our gain.

Last of the Water Muses?

It is not surprising that the beauty of the wetlands should have inspired some of our most famous poets. Alfred Lord Tennyson was born on the northern edge of the Fens, in the Lincolnshire village of Somersby. What childhood encounter with the marshes and rivers of his home, what romantic river landscapes did he encounter as a student at Cambridge that led him to compose lines like those of 'The Lady of Shalott'?

> Willows whiten, aspens quiver
> Little breezes dusk and shiver
> Thro' the wave that runs forever
> By the island in the river . . .
>
> By the margin, willow-veil'd,
> Slide the heavy barges trail'd
> By slow horses; and unhail'd
> The shallop flitteth silken-sail'd.

Byron and Brooke were also at Cambridge. Byron wrote a poem about his experience there, 'Granta'. Rupert Brooke lived for a time at the Old Vicarage in Grantchester by the singing river. He loved the waters and the calm, and perhaps it was these magic wet places he was thinking of when he wrote the immortal tragic lines that culminated in 'If I should die, think only this of me':

> Dawn was theirs,
>   And sunset, and the colours of the earth
> These had seen movement, and heard music: known
>   Slumber and waking; loved; gone proudly friended
> Felt the quick stir of wonder; sat alone;
>   Touched flowers and furs and cheeks.'

The message is plain: lose our wetland landscapes and we lose forever the chance of further poetic wonder.

The Last Ditch Stand

Man has been present in East Anglia since the ice sheets went into final meltdown 10,000 years ago. But simple agriculture and low population densities meant that our impact was minimal, that we were still being controlled by our environment, suffering along with all our fellow animals the harsh winters, droughts, floods and other disasters that nature visited upon us.

Gradually our slow and painstaking activities began to influence the world around us. More and more trees disappeared, grazing regimes created pasture – some years wetter than others – but pastureland nonetheless. Even the majestic Broads themselves are the direct result of our forebears' activities as they cut and dried the peat that

provided heat and cooking fires. The origins of flower-rich meadows can be traced back to the Middle Ages through particular agricultural and drainage practices.

Through time, as East Anglian man has prospered and multiplied, so his effect on the wetlands around him has become more manifest. He has had more money to spend on drainage, to rid the Fens of pestilence and to make room for more intensive farming. But it hasn't been quite as simple as that. Pestilence was as much the result of poor sanitation than of the supposedly ague-ridden marshes, and the improvements began to go awry. In the Fens, the land began to shrink as it dried, and as it dried, it cracked and oxidized.

In 1848 the Holme Post, a huge metal gauge, was sunk into the fertile Fenland soil at Holme in order to measure the state of peat shrinkage in the Fens. New drains and land use around the post increased compaction, shrinkage and oxidization of the peat, and the land began to sink at an average of 3cm a year. Over the ensuing years the post has emerged to stand four metres proud of the surrounding land. Of course this shrinkage has led to problems. Rivers and drains now flow above surrounding farmland, and powerful energy-guzzling pumps are required to remove water from fields. European Community agricultural funds provide grants to assist in this drainage, and during the 1980s over one million pounds was spent on a single pumping station at March, solely to counter the effects of this peat shrinkage.

What price now, our draining of the wetlands? The real costs

may never be known because of the complexity and scale of the issues at stake. The Nature Conservancy Council has estimated that between 1637 and 1984 over 3,000 square kilometres of East Anglian fenland was destroyed. Today less than ten square kilometres of this unique habitat remain and none of this can be regarded as being in its natural state. This means a loss to agriculture, drainage and man of over 99 per cent of total fenland. With this loss of habitat goes the wildlife – the Norfolk aeshna dragonfly, swallowtail butterfly, otter, bittern, milk parsley and marsh pea are all teetering on the brink of local extinction.

However, there is now increasing national concern for the East Anglian wetlands and the appreciation of wetland value has never been greater. Much of the Broads are for example now afforded statutory protection under national legislation. International recognition also plays its part, with the designation of four of East Anglia's most noteworthy wetland sites within the Ramsar Convention.

Wetlands are the only ecosystem to be accorded their own conservation convention, named after the town of Ramsar in Iran where the aims and policies of this unique legislation were given flesh and body. The main aims of the convention are to stem the worldwide decline in wetlands and to maintain their ecological functions and value to wildlife and to people. Those Anglian sites singled out for protection by this auspicious world gathering were Hickling Broad and Horsey Mere, the North Norfolk Coast, the Ouse Washes and the Bure Marshes.

Two recent watersheds in Anglian wetland history stand out. The first was the bitterly fought battle of Halvergate Marshes in the early eighties which led to the marshes being designated an Environmentally Sensitive Area (see page 151). Following fairly close behind, and partly as a result of this confrontation, the Broads were confirmed as a designated National Park. This achievement was all the more remarkable considering the huge number of divergent vested interests that laid claim to some part of Broadland heritage.

Perhaps it is the lot of the Broads as the heartland of the Anglian wetlands that, after centuries as backwaters of concern, they should be thrust into the limelight as a result of conflicting interests: the flotillas of windsurfers and pleasure boat owners; the 'green' visitors who tick off the bittern, the milk parsley and the dragonflies; the farming interests who strive to make a living from a shrinking resource and an environment where political goalposts move almost as much as the swaying reeds.

Everyone expects something from the Broads, and the accommodation of such diverse tastes will certainly prove a challenging and onerous task. However, the challenge has somehow to be met. Through carelessness, we have already lost so much of our wetland wilderness. We cannot afford to lose the rest.

A Wetland Journey

Join us in a quick tour of England's lost wetlands, an exploration by car, boat, foot and train of the main sights and sounds of the East Anglian wetlands, the Broads, fens and coastal marshes. Our route is a circular one, like all good walks anywhere, but it may not be the kind of tour that you would wish to do all in one go. We suggest instead that you dip into this for ideas of where to go if you want to experience this magical wetland world at first hand. If however you are armchair bound, dip lightly into the text, close your eyes, imagine the sounds of curlews and a vision of waving reeds: lean back and think of England's lost wetland wilderness.

From Grantchester to Brancaster

And where better to think of England than in Grantchester, among the meadows, verdant green, buzzing with bees, a playground for Cambridge students, tourists and anglers. Home too, to fish, fowl and mammal. This quiet corner has come to represent the essence of everything that is English. Here the First World War poet Rupert Brooke lodged as a Cambridge undergraduate, initially at The Orchard and later at The Old Vicarage.

> There's peace and holy quiet there,
> Great clouds along pacific skies,
> And men and women with straight eyes,
> Lithe children lovelier than a dream,
> A bosky wood, a slumbrous stream,
> And little kindly winds that creep
> Round twilight corners, half asleep.
>
> RUPERT BROOKE, *The Old Vicarage, Grantchester*

Brooke's time at Grantchester was an idyllic time in his life: 'I work at Shakespeare, read, write all day, and now and then wander in the woods by the river.' Later his nostalgia for Grantchester became immortalized in that classic line: 'Is there honey still for tea?'

No time for honey and nostalgia now, for we must set sail

Keeping watch over the Fens: Ely Cathedral.

on the first leg of our tour, away from the cosiness of Grantchester to the wild coast of North Norfolk. The route is by boat down the Cam, taking a passing glance at the majestic architecture along the Backs of the Cambridge colleges, and being careful to avoid the wayward punts with their cargoes of bright young things.

But before joining the Great Ouse at Ely, take a detour along Wicken Lode, an ancient man-made waterway, once a major artery for carrying crops across the Fens, now used only by pleasure craft. The Lode is a direct route to Wicken Fen, Britain's first nature reserve, an island of conservation and natural diversity amid a sea of intensive monocrop agriculture.

The island city of Ely is where we must say goodbye to the Cam, which flows into the Great Ouse to the south. All views of Ely are dominated by its famous cathedral, rising up from the flat surrounding Fens, tall and stately and true to its title, the 'ship of the Fens'. Imagine the scene 900 years ago when Ely was an island haven amid the morass of the surrounding hostile fen. Here, mighty Hereward the Wake made his stand against William the Conqueror.

Pause only for a moment, because King's Lynn beckons. This ancient Anglian trading port sits astride the Great Ouse as it flows sluggishly north parallel to the Old and New Bedford Rivers. The Fens around here are characterized by straight, parallel lines, parcelling up the land into regimented packages. The Old and New Bedford Rivers cut an uncompromising

swathe through the landscape, a remnant of the drainage efforts of Cornelius Vermuyden in the seventeenth century.

Little did the Dutchman know that his mighty engineering efforts were to bequeath what is today one of the most spectacular wildlife sights in the region: the Hundred Foot Washes. Lying between the Old and New Bedford Rivers, the Washes are a haven for thousands of birds. Here Sir Peter Scott's Wildfowl Trust founded the Welney Wildfowl Refuge. If you stop for tea at the Welney Centre, raise your china to Vermuyden by all means, but remember also to toast Sir Peter, the father of conservation, without whom our world

Wisbech.

would be a sorrier place, with much less trust in and understanding of its wildfowl.

The Great Ouse meets the two great Bedford Rivers near the village of Denver where another monument to man's engineering persistence stands – Denver sluice. It was built originally in the seventeenth century, but had to be replaced a century later when it failed to hold up against bad flooding.

At King's Lynn we must abandon the boat and continue by car down the A149, past Castle Rising, with one of the biggest Norman keeps in the country, and on to Snettisham, not forgetting a curious glance as you pass Sandringham, the Norfolk home of the Royal Family.

Snettisham, and Titchwell further round the coast, are R S P B reserves, famed for their winter wildfowl population. Feast your eyes on the spectacular sight of tens of thousands of wading birds congregating on the reserve to escape the peak high tides. Eighty thousand knot, one of our more endearing little wading birds, were counted in one morning at Snettisham. Pick the right day and you could even see 10,000 oystercatchers, 10,000 dunlin, 2,000 shelduck and 1,000 grey plover, give or take the odd duck or two.

The road follows the curve of the Wash to Hunstanton and on to Holme next the Sea where the energetic can leave the car behind and carry on by way of the Norfolk Coast Path which threads its way through nature reserve country. This is still prime birdwatcher country. In fact, the birders even have

their own telephone line, 'Bird Line', which can give you the latest hot tips on which bird is roosting where.

The vast tracts of tidal mudflats which melt muddily into the sea on this northern angle of England's wetland give this section of the North Norfolk coastline a magical, semi-real aura. It looks like uncharted territory, ever-changing as the sands shift and the sea carves out its new channels through the mud. Spend a summer evening on the sands north of Holme next the Sea and know that you live. The sun setting red on the wet flats will pick out not just feathered flights in twilight abundance but prawn netters beyond the first rollers, and sylph-like swimmers treading water and catching sun shadows on the waters.

The coastal environs of Brancaster village can be wild. Walk towards the beach from the village and you can have no notion of what lies hidden behind the uniform bank of sand dunes. Venture through the gap and the full roar of the North Sea hits you with a massive force as it pounds the shore. Struggle along the beach a little way if you can, sinking into the fine shifting sand and imagine what it must have been like for the Roman soldiers posted to the fort which lies just off the coast path. Nothing but a square of raised ground now remains of Branodunum, but it must have been a bleak, cruel posting in the depths of a raw winter.

Across the mudflats a little further on is Scolt Head Island, putty in the hands of the mighty sea which continually moulds the sand and shingle, changing its shape. At low tide

it looks tempting to strike out across the mudflats and walk to the island, a nature reserve managed by the Nature Conservancy Council. But be warned; you need local knowledge to pick the right route. Find a friendly boatman at Brancaster Staithe who will take you out.

For sheer natural beauty, walk a little further, take a deep breath and savour the unrivalled sight of Holkham Bay. The sea seems to disappear beyond the horizon and the uninterrupted sky broods restlessly over the scene. Walk inland and you'll find Holkham Hall, a Palladian mansion set in parkland designed by Capability Brown. It is the home of the Coke family, descendants of Thomas Coke of Norfolk, the

eighteenth-century agricultural improver who used new crops and introduced sheep instead of cattle at Holkham to improve productivity.

From Wells to Wroxham, by train

Time for a detour. At Wells Next the Sea, but no longer next to the sea because of massive sand deposition, you can catch the light railway to Little Walsingham. This is a fascinating village which in summer is the destination of thousands of pilgrims who journey to the shrine of Our Lady of Walsingham. It was once such a famous pilgrimage that people would call the

Holkham Hall (opposite).

Off the beaten track: the Wells/Walsingham Light Railway (right).

Milky Way the Walsingham Way. Near Walsingham is Warham Camp, one of Norfolk's best preserved Iron Age hill forts, thought to have been built round the first century BC.

Off the tracks and back up north on the coast path again, our route weaves towards Blakeney, a village which sums up the essence of North Norfolk. The energetic can walk to Blakeney Point, but infinitely more fun are the boat trips. The fishing boats, laden to the gunwales with camera-clicking tourists, chug up the channel towards the sand spit of Blakeney Point. This is home to a large population of watery-eyed common seals, though sadly now they are not as common as they once were.

A gull's cry from Blakeney is Cley nature reserve, run by the Norfolk Naturalists' Trust. It was here that a group of forward-thinking ornithologists established the nature reserve which was to herald the formation of the Norfolk Naturalists' Trust, the first county wildlife trust in the country.

From now on the coastline is dominated by cliffs, formed from Ice Age debris, which are being constantly eroded by sea and wind. Centuries of this erosion swept the village of Shipden into the sea, and even now threatens to wash away the clifftop golf course . . . Fore below! What would the people of this area not give for some of the sand and mud which so happily settles on the land further back along the coast, choking up old waterways and making the sea something of a distant force?

People are wont to fall in love with Sheringham and Cromer. Their unassuming manner, that slight hint of decayed elegance

and a distinct lack of overt money-spinning consumerism makes people return there time and time again for something more than just the whelks and cockles and the kiss-me-quick hats.

What better way to travel on the next section of the journey but by train either from Cromer in the north or Norwich in the south to the gateway of the Broads – Wroxham? We think of railways as being slow olde-worlde ways of getting about, but when they first came to Norfolk they changed for ever the character of Broadland. The age of steam opened up the Broads to a genteel crowd of middle- and upper-class Edwardian families in search of a bit of wilderness, open space and sunshine. As holidays became the right of all, thousands of working people relished the chance to get behind the wheel of a boat, and piled onto holiday express trains to head for the Broads. Today still sees Norwich station in the middle of summer awash with travellers searching for the Wroxham train.

Alight from the train at Wroxham today and you might think you've got off at the wrong stop. Where, you may well ask, are the tranquillity, the scenery, and the wide expanses of water everyone has been telling you about? You can see only a lot of traffic and a huge complex called 'Roy's of Wroxham', known as the biggest village store in the world, but really a supermarket which has outgrown its origins.

Wroxham station is actually in Hoveton. These two villages lie cheek-by-jowl, an uneasy truce between them. Wroxham gets all the publicity but ends as soon as you have crossed the river bridge. But before we go aboard our boat we suggest

The first real taste of open water is Wroxham Broad, a tree-fringed broad with plenty of wind for the experts, and enough space for the novices to keep out of the way. It is always colourful, but Wroxham Broad takes on a carnival atmosphere during regatta week, one of the high points on the river social scene.

The river Bure then sweeps round in a deep curve, skirting Hoveton Great Broad and Salhouse Broad. The latter may not be the most stunning of Broads, but it clearly shows the problem of bank erosion. Instead of a reed-fringed sloping edge, there is a muddy shoreline. The geese and ducks which congregate there give anything that might try to colonize the bank little chance of success.

As the river turns north once again, Decoy Broad is on the right, close to Woodbastwick Marshes. A little further and you reach Hoveton Little Broad. Little it may be, but it was once the scene of a bitter battle. It was one historic Friday in March 1949 when a fleet of craft, including a wherry and a houseboat, made a full sail assault on Hoveton Little to assert the ancient rights of the waterways. No doubt they were castigated at the time as hooligans and troublemakers. But are we not glad they did?

According to the story, Black Horse Broad, as it is commonly known, was then owned by farmer Tom Blofeld, father of the cricket commentator Henry Blofeld. Tom had blocked the entry of the Broad with thirty wooden piles. The invading party, led by fleet owner Herbert Woods, hauled the mighty

that you take a detour by car up the B1354 towards Coltishall. Today Coltishall is a small, pretty village and it marks the end of navigation on the Bure. But a century ago it was a Victorian boom town with nine pubs, many craftsmen, a railway station, cattle market and a major malting industry. It was credited with being the birthplace of the wherry, the huge black-sailed trading vessels of the Broads.

By Boat at Last: Down the Bure

You can take a comfortable little cabin cruiser from any one of a number of boatyards in Wroxham, follow the speed limits and the bends in the river, and forge your own pathway down into the heart of England's wetland wilderness. Here you are in a magic astral land of reeds, of grebe, swan, coot and swallow, of wind and windmill. It is another world, another time, another place.

Atop the boardwalk: Cockshoot Dyke (opposite).

Keeping wildlife afloat: the floating conservation centre, Ranworth Broad (below).

Overleaf: Here's leaning at yew kid! Ranworth Church (left).

The view from Ranworth Church (right).

tree trunks from their resting place and sailed onto the broad toasting their success with beer furnished by the houseboat.

It was a stunt, but it was a stunt that was meant to reverberate around the Broads in a bid to settle the question of private and public water, an issue that Herbert Woods thought vital if the holiday industry was to press ahead. The Black Horse case ended up in the Chancery division of the High Court, and was eventually settled in favour of the watermen.

Sail on, and the Bure carves through the middle of the village of Horning, a honeypot for the day trippers. Leaving Horning, the river passes through what can only be described as Broadland suburbs before coming out amid the open farming and grazing land near Ranworth. Be sure and disembark at Cockshoot Broad and follow the boardwalk to this magnificently restored stretch of water. Be patient for long enough in the hide and you might even catch a glimpse of a delicate Chinese water deer.

Malthouse and Ranworth Broads lie side by side but could not be more different. Malthouse is the public, holiday face of Broadland, teeming with cruisers, sails, row boats, windsurfers and obliging ducks waiting to be fed. Ranworth Broad harks back to another age. It belongs to the Norfolk Naturalists' Trust and is closed to navigation. To get to it, follow a boardwalk to the thatched floating conservation centre which tells the story of the Broads and gives spectacular views across the water, home to wetland wildlife of all shapes and sizes. Boardwalking over the marsh is an interesting experience; it really brings home the swamp-like atmosphere of the wetlands. It is an ancient experience too: the only way that the ancient Fenlanders could get from place to place across the marshes was on raised boardwalks, or on stilts.

Ranworth Church is known as the cathedral of the Broads. It is famous for the fifteenth-century screen with paintings of the twelve apostles and other saints. Their faces, feet and hands have been painted over and destroyed, probably by Puritan zealots but this does not detract from their vibrancy and richness. It is worth climbing the church tower because it gives one of the best views over the Bure.

Every village worth its salt has a ghost, and Ranworth is no

exception. It is said that the wraith of Colonel Sidney walks abroad after he mysteriously disappeared from the Old Hall in Ranworth on New Year's Eve 1770. When he disappeared the hall was handsomely furnished. According to Ranworth village's guidebook, it was left for seven years; 'the silken curtains rotted at the broken windows, the furniture dropped to pieces in the stately rooms; the birds built their nests on the top of the beautifully carved oaken bedsteads.' Advertisements for the missing Colonel met with no response and the property was sold.

Back on the boat and it's time for another detour, this time up the River Ant, hard work if you're unlucky enough to be quanting a wherry round the narrow curves and sharp bends, but well worth the effort. Take good care under Ludham Bridge,

for there's not much margin for error. A few miles and a lot of twists and turns further on is How Hill, a beautiful house with a remarkable history.

This stunning turn-of-the-century building, once the home of the Boardman family, now an environmental centre, must command one of the best views in the area. The 365-acre estate is a microcosm of Broadland with reed-beds, marshes, a small broad, woodlands, a reach of the River Ant, restored marsh mills and a tiny cottage, once the home of a marshman. That is before you ever take into account the gardens which impress even the most reluctant gardeners.

The house was built by Edward Thomas Boardman who was the son of leading architect Edward Boardman, founder of the family firm which was to design many of the beautiful buildings of Norwich, and worked on the conversion of Norwich Castle from a prison into a museum. Edward Thomas became head of the family firm in 1900. In 1898 he had married Florence Esther Colman, a match which united two of the leading county families and made lots of mustard to boot.

How Hill became a happy lively family home. Shooting and fishing played a major part in life on the estate, with the estate records revealing such famous names as Peter Scott and the Duke of Grafton joining the shooting parties. Good shooting required good conservation. When the shooting dwindled, the wetland management went with it; the fabric of the marshland ecosystem began to break up.

The house was sold in 1966 and became a county-council-

owned residential centre where thousands of school-children came to stay to learn about the landscape. Spending cuts brought that to an end, but thankfully, today it is in good hands, being run by a trust. Schoolchildren, students, ordinary members of the public know How Hill as the environmental centre for the Broads. One curiosity not to be missed on your visit is Hitler's Oak, clearly marked at the end of the nature trail. It was given to Christopher Boardman for his gold medal success in sailing in the Berlin Olympics and was planted in the grounds in September 1936.

Continue north on the Ant towards Barton Broad, a vast popular piece of water, which seems to defy all attempts to restore its water quality. Keep an eye open for the cormorants who perch hauntingly on the channel markers.

We rejoin the Bure where we left it. Fleet Dyke will take you to South Walsham Broad, which consists of an inner and an outer Broad. You can moor on the outer, but the inner remains something of a haven. Its tranquillity was rudely shattered on Whit Monday 1901 when war of sorts was declared on South Walsham Broad. It seems that the owner had put up posts and wire across the stretch of water dividing the inner from the outer broad. This enraged locals who gathered on the staithe to make their protest.

The owner promptly moored his houseboat, *The Ark*, near the entrance and it seemed from a distance to be armed to the teeth with guns and 'men of formidable appearance'. But in fact the armament was one small hand-operated fire engine, and what villagers thought to be the Vickers Maxim machine-gun was nothing more threatening than the highly-polished barrel of an old telescope. The villagers, well plied with beer, knew when they were beaten. Peace was declared and no blows were struck. But the right of way was restored to the villagers. Access through the channel was allowed, providing they did not go ashore. That rule remains to this day. No mooring, fishing, nor swimming is allowed. Thus a glorious tranquil stretch of water remains undisturbed.

Visitors to the churchyard in South Walsham might be forgiven for doing a double take. There are in fact two churches side by side in the same churchyard, although one has now lost its tower and fallen into disrepair. According to legend, two local sisters disagreed over the plans for a church on their jointly owned patch of land, and so each went ahead with her own design. But the real reason is far more practical. It is thought that the boundary between two adjoining manors met where the churchyard is now. And as this was the firmest and highest ground around, both owners chose the site for their place of worship.

But places of worship are not confined to the villages in this area. St Bene't's Abbey on the Bure, opposite Fleet Dyke, has been a landmark on the Broads for over 1,000 years. Its few remaining ruins, some of which lurk hauntingly just below the river waters close to the bank, are now a mere shadow of their former glory, when the monks who lived there commanded the respect of those around (see page 127).

Thurne, Thurne and Bure Again

It is time now for another detour, up the river Thurne. Once you reach Potter Heigham, described by one Broads writer a little harshly as a 'bungaloid slum', there is a distinct change. Potter Heigham Bridge seems to act as a barrier. Many holidaymakers turn round at this point to head for the bright lights of the southern Broads. Beyond the bridge the way seems more desolate, less friendly, but nonetheless rewarding. For it is the gateway to the wildest and biggest of the Broads, Hickling, and to Horsey Mere, so close to the North Sea that you can almost hear the waves pounding the sea defences. For many, this somewhat isolated quarter of the Broads is unrivalled for peace and a sense of solitude.

Horsey Mere has long been a stranded area of Broadland. For many years there were little more than cart tracks for roads around Somerton and Horsey. In Roman times the whole area which we now know as Broadland was a great estuary which the Romans called Gariensis. The sea ebbed and flowed through four great mouths, one of which was at Horsey. All that remains of this sea inlet is a miserable-looking ditch known as the Hundred Stream.

Villagers used to speak of the time when 'The king's navy rode on the Old Hundred Stream and mark you, one day ships will ride there again!' It seems laughable when you look at the Hundred Stream today, but on several occasions it almost looked like coming true. Horsey is the most vulnerable point for flooding for the whole Broads. Time and time again over the centuries the sand-hills have been breached by tides.

The Broads suffered the worst flood this century on Saturday 31 January 1953 when the North Sea hurled itself at the East Coast with a ferocity not experienced in living memory. In total, 307 people died, 400 houses were completely destroyed and 32,000 people were forced to leave their homes as the water poured in. The highest death toll was at Hunstanton and Snettisham where 65 people drowned.

Back to the present, and to Martham, which is in many ways the forgotten stretch of the river. For as long as men have been farming the marshes on the Hickling side of the river, there has been a ferry at Martham.

G. Christopher Davies, the author whom many people credit with 'discovering' the Broads, encountered the ferry when sailing on the Thurne in the 1880s, and described how wherrymen would run their wherries full tilt against it. Today the farm which owns and maintains the ferry has no such problems. But to work the ferry, farmworkers still have to haul on a long chain to pull it across the river.

We rejoin the river Bure at Thurne itself, where the river sweeps south. A long dyke leading to the village of Upton is worth exploring because it is here that the trading wherry *Maud* is being restored. Next stop is Acle where the bridge proves a natural barrier for those not tempted to head to Yarmouth. But it might be an idea to avoid Acle Bridge on the night of 7 April. For this is when a gruesome murder is

said to be re-enacted. Late at night, a man is supposed to
lean against the wall of the bridge only to be attacked by a
huge live skeleton glowing with uncanny light. The skeleton
stabs the man, forcing his head back over the bridge. The two
disappear and there is no trace of the violence except fresh
blood all over the stone. The story goes back to one Josiah
Burge who beat his wife to death but was acquitted after a
trial at Norwich. The brother of the woman learnt of the
murder and took revenge on Burge before escaping. Someone
else swung for the crime, but the real murderer returned to the
scene of his deed. The skeleton which sprung out and
murdered him is said to be that of the innocent victim who
hung for Burge's murder.

Yare In, Yare Out

Our journey down the Bure ends here but the Bure carries on to Yarmouth. In the past it swept north and went into the sea by the Roman port of Caister. There is no navigable connection between the rivers Bure and Yare, so you either have to walk or fly or, more poetically, take a train or car west to Norwich and the start of a second river trip, down the Yare.

Norwich, the capital of Norfolk, is a fine city with an imposing yet elegant cathedral, some nice waterside walks and old streets, and a traffic congestion problem which defies the best laid plans of mice, men and the town planners. In earlier, wetter times, the Tas, a tributary of the Yare, which runs south of Norwich City would have been large enough to have allowed Roman galleys to sail down to Venta Icenorum, the then county town. All that remains today of the Roman presence is a raised rectangular area with a ruined wall within which stands the church of Caistor St Edmund's.

As you sail down the Yare, cast a reverent eye at Surlingham Broad. This is known as the wherry graveyard, for here at low tide it is possible to see some of the decaying hulls of wherries sunk in Surlingham at their working lives' end.

A little way down is Strumpshaw Fen, an RSPB reserve where some innovative work has been undertaken to create a haven which still retains a wilderness feel and where the hand of conservation management is altogether more subtle than in the high-profile reserves on the North Norfolk coast.

Industry looms further downriver in the shape of the British Sugar factory at Cantley. The sweet sickly smell from the sugar beet plant permeates across the marshes, even as far as Reedham. But there's no time to dally, for there's a train to catch at Reedham. It is only a short journey to Yarmouth, but it is a journey that cuts through the heart of huge tracts of grazing marshes and skirts the edge of Breydon Water. There is just one stop, at Berney Arms, so remote that passengers have to make a special request to alight there, and when they want to catch a train back to civilization they have to flag it down.

It's an engaging ride; the sheep, cattle and horses barely notice the passing of the train, but the lapwings and other birds feeding on the marshes launch into flight as the tiny train trundles by. Derelict windpumps in various stages of decay stand as monuments to the past; the dykes, glinting in the sunlight, serve instead of fences as barriers between the fields. When the train reaches the southern end of Breydon Water, turn and look back across the mud and sand flats and contemplate the wild expanse of water stretching before your eyes, where flocks of birds wheel and dive, before the train plods into the outskirts of the station where once again industry and commerce break the wilderness spell.

The next section of our tour calls for a bit of leg stretching. Leaving the train, walk over the mighty Breydon Bridge, and follow the footpath along the south bank of Breydon Water to Burgh Castle. Stand to attention when you reach the site of the

Roman fort which commands a magnificent view across the river and marshes beyond. Burgh Castle, then called Gariennonum, was built during the third century AD as part of the defensive chain guarding the east coast from Saxon raiders.

Where Winds the Waveney

Burgh Castle brings us to the third great Broadland waterway, the river Waveney, where it is time to get afloat once again. The Waveney is a lovely, perhaps underrated river but it too has its murkier side. Historian Walter Rye tells of a scoundrel on the River Waveney who murdered his sweetheart. He weighted her body and sunk it in a creek, then took to keeping an eel-set hard by so as to profit by his ghastly ground bait. It is said he bequeathed it to a nephew who let the story out when drunk one night at the King's Arms, Beccles.

At St Olave's it is possible to take a short-cut back to Reedham via the New Cut. In fact it is not so new; it was actually built in 1832 to save precious time for wherries heading for Reedham and avoiding Yarmouth.

Somerleyton is known for its Hall which in turn is famous for its maze, a deceptively easy-looking puzzle which has been known to catch out the unwary. So if you're not stuck in the maze, carry on down the Waveney and take the dyke which leads to Oulton Broad, once described as the 'most civilized of all the Broads'. It is now a leisure Broad where windsurfing is popular, and the cafés and restaurants make it a 'bright lights' tourist spot, but it has not lost its charm of eighty years ago.

Beccles, further on, could never lose its charm. Many might say it has not been tainted by the Broads traffic. The town is a thriving community with a soul of its own so has no need to sell it to the holiday industry. Navigation on the Waveney is here all but ended, but it is possible to go as far as Geldeston where you can drown your sorrows or joys in Geldeston Locks pub, accessible only on foot and by boat.

We are now forced to continue by car, but the route along the A143 follows as nearly as possible the course of the Waveney as it meanders through the valley, leaving wide open plains on either bank. After Bungay, turn off the main road as signposted to the Otter Trust, where, if you've time, there is a rare opportunity to see otters in a semi-natural environment.

The Trust was set up by notable conservation enthusiast Philip Wayre to bring about a revival of the fortunes of one of Britain's most charming animals, now sadly a threatened species. It has had significant success in re-introducing otters bred in captivity to the wild. In 1984, history was made when it was discovered that the newly introduced otters had successfully bred and reared cubs in the wild. The Trust aims to release more otters each year until this engaging creature is once again firmly established in the country's waterways.

Rejoin the A143 towards Harleston, but turn off left and go through the village of Wortwell. On the crown of a sharp right-hand bend, where the Bell pub stands, fork left down a

small by-road called the Low Road. This weaves its way prettily through the Waveney Valley to Weybread and back on the main road through to Diss.

The medieval poet John Skelton was rector of Diss in the early 1500s. 'Dis' was the Latin name for the Underworld and King Henry VII is reputed to have taken great pleasure in referring to Skelton as his Rector of Hell. Diss is probably best known for its Mere which is supposed to be as deep as the church tower is tall, and that's pretty deep. Like all the local meres it is fed by chalk springs. There must be something in the water because the mere is home to some of the best fed and fattest ducks in Norfolk.

Leave Diss on the A1066 and at South Lopham turn left on the B1113 to Redgrave where lurks a nature reserve called Redgrave Fen. Here, if you knew which squelch of mud to look for, you could find the source of both the Waveney, which we have just followed, and the Little Ouse which we're about to follow.

Easily Back to the Ouse

Follow the network of minor roads towards Thelnetham, crossing the B1111 at Hopton, and you're heading for Knettishall Heath and Breckland. The gently rolling fields of the Waveney Valley are now all behind; instead the dry, chalky soil of Breckland gives rise to heathland and scrub, perhaps not so aesthetically pleasing but nonetheless an important habitat for wildlife.

Thetford beckons, once one of England's major cities, with the remains of its castle mound and priory. Here in 1737 Tom Paine, author of the revolutionary pamphlet *The Rights of Man* and architect of independent America, was born. Seven miles north-west of Thetford is the oldest industrial site in Europe, where neolithic man mined flint 4,000 years ago. About 500 shafts were sunk here with deer antlers used as picks to prise out the flint from the chalk. Centuries later, the nearby town of Brandon was to become the country's flint capital. During the Napoleonic Wars there were probably as many as 200 knappers working in the town, fashioning tinder and gun flints.

Flint predominates in East Anglian architecture and can be seen in every kind of building from a common garden wall to the most beautiful of churches. But it is not easy to make good, strong corners with natural flint, which may be one reason why so many of East Anglia's early churches have round towers.

For purists who like a tour to finish more or less where it began, the course of the Little Ouse twists and turns out of the Brecks to the Fens until it meets up with the Great Ouse just north of the town of Littleport, which isn't far north of where we came in. And now that you've been with us on a journey through space, how about coming on a journey through time, back to the beginning of England's wetland world?

Out of the Mists

The Crystal Dawn

In the beginning of the geological age in which we live there was another kind of wetland altogether, a wetland without swamp marsh, fen or even standing water. This was the Ice Time. East Anglia was a land of frozen waters, of ice, great unbroken sheets of it, extending well into the land masses of Eastern England and the continental shelf. Where there was no ice proper, to the south, there was ice tundra, a periglacial winter-scape of frozen ice-packed earth.

Imagine standing on the ice-cap some 15,000 years ago and seeing nothing at first but a great white shimmering desert, the crystal ice sparkling brilliantly in the sunshine. But in the distance, gaps in the ice provide darker vistas of glacial tills and moraines, offering plants a foothold in this bleak and barren land. It was on this skeleton of young, mineral-rich soils that life began the long haul back, fingers of tundra insinuating themselves into the melting ice. Patches of arctic vegetation appeared as if by magic along with a hardy flower or two, a cloud of insects, some birds and the odd ice-mammal. There may have been some people too, but not many, and as hunters living off the ice-edge pickings, they had little significant impact on the environment. The time of the people had not really come, and it did not materialize until many more years had passed.

Before this crystal dawn, there were, of course, other beginnings. But as far as our story goes, the melting of the ice was the important one: it was from the glacial debris and meltwaters that were formed the first rivers and swamps that shaped the East Anglian landscapes we know today. The melting of the ice left behind the low-lying plain of Eastern England, of which East Anglia forms the flattest parts. This plain, made up of clays and gravel, sand and chalky drift, roughly occupies an area between the two belts of chalk and limestone that run across England from the Humber in the north to the Chilterns in the south.

The chalk which underlies the Breckland and the glacial and fluvial subsoils of the Broads, and outcrops towards the coast most spectacularly at the cliffs of Cromer, is the very oldest rock in the region. This was laid down when there was nothing here but sea, in Mesozoic times, between 225 and 65 million years ago. This was an age of sea serpents, of great reptiles like sea lizards or enaliosaurs, and the pterodactyls, not dinosaurs but just as terrible. The chalk was formed out of the remains of much smaller things, of minute sea creatures, single-celled foraminifoa, layer upon layer compressed by their accumulating weight. The whole mass of lime, washed over and over by unpolluted seas, came out bright white, except for the odd whole yellowish flint nodule and of course the fossils – galleries and galleries of them.

Later geological eras brought retreating seas and emerging lands to the west, with the might of enormous rivers rolling the chalk and flint into pebbles, grinding and re-sorting them into mud. The Eocene age 50 million years ago brought with it a new warmth. The seas and the land swarmed with animals and the shores of East Anglia were crowded with crocodiles and turtles taking shade under whole forests of bananas, palms and other tropical trees.

Those luxuriant times didn't last. Later eras brought more temperate conditions, and some fascinating bits of geological change. At one time an even mightier Rhine flowed over Eastern England, carving out the Channel and depositing Rhine muds all over the area. This was when a great forest covered the land, complete with elephants, hippos and sabre-toothed cats. But it wasn't all exotica and Rhine Maiden muds: there arrived also familiar tree cover, of Scots pine, oak and alder, stretches of marsh and freshwater lake, frequented by otter, heron, grebe and vole. Water lilies graced the shrinking pools. The marshes were gay with cotton grass and meadow rue, and wet meadows sparkled with golden buttercups. This was the archetypal wetland, of a kind we long for today, rich with a diversity of plantlife, and flock upon flock of wild birds.

Then with the advent of the more recent Pleistocene era, between 2 million and 10,000 years ago, the climate grew colder – not much, but enough. Great glaciers issuing forth from the Scandinavian fjords extended their cold death across the North Sea and the Anglian Rhinelands. At one time, one single ice sheet, the Great Eastern Glacier, descended through Lincolnshire and spread its weight and its deposits of chalky boulder clay right through central East Anglia and the southern fens down into the Thames Valley.

It seems likely that the main river valleys of East Anglia were cut during one particular period of ice advance, when the land lay bent and warped under the great weight of grumbling groaning ice slowly moving above. One glacier in particular is known to have moved down the valley of the Yare, eastwards of Norwich. As this and the other glaciers melted, they shrank into the Broadland valleys, eroding and deepening them, and filling them with boulder clay. Eventually, when the warmth returned and the ice retreated, the meltwaters completed the carving out of the East Anglian landscapes we know today.

This brings us back to where we started, back to the end of the last advance of ice, for the glacial epoch consisted of not one, but many buildups and meltdowns – and we're still in there, still in the grip of the Ice Time. Modern man exists by courtesy of a warmer interglacial between one Ice Age and another; our epoch is only the latest warm bit between the white sheets of ice which, regardless of any greenhouse effect, will one day return again.

The Return of the Sea

The chalk ridge which runs from Lincolnshire through Hunstanton and into the North Norfolk Coast, eroded by the action of ice and rivers, proved an ineffectual barrier against the return of the salt water. The sea flooded in at various times between 1300 and 300 BC, until eventually the Wash finally became a permanent feature on the modern map, a great wet bite out of Anglia's eastern side. North, south and west of this, silt and sand blown on inshore winds and carried ashore by the highest tides met the sand and silt brought down by the Anglian rivers, and an inland sea was formed. In time, this silted up, with deposits from the rivers on one side, and the tides on the other. Land levels gradually rose while the sea stayed put, and so the Fens were formed, occupying an area of some 3,800 square kilometres around the Wash.

So what is fen? Fen is primary temperate wetland, not swamp, not water meadow, but a magic in-between phenomenon, a rich and complex habitat supporting communities of herbs, grasses and sedges that all like to keep their feet wet. The ground is springy and spongy and the rich ground-water, here charged with lime, supports a wealth of green growth full of flowers. This in turn supports an enormous insect population which in turn feed a diversity of wild birds and fish.

Much of the area occupied by fenland today was colonized during drier, warmer times by vast wildwoods of pine and birch. As the climate became warmer, oak, lime, alder and beech took root, with aurochs and wild boar living within the shelter of their trunks.

In time the climate got wetter again, and so did the wetland landscape. The waterlogged trees keeled over and collapsed, as new swampy mossy vegetation grew up to take their place. Many years later, when the Fens were drained, some of these well-preserved trees had a second lease of life, as 'bog oaks', used for church carvings and furniture.

In time the new vegetation of this once-extensive landscape turned into peat: a substance that forms the very heart of fenland past and present, Anglian or otherwise.

The Message in the Peat

Peat is decayed organic matter, mainly of plant origin – bits of stems, roots, leaves, flowers, fruits and pollen grains – and also the harder bits of beetles, bugs and other insects.

So, to the experts who can identify these living remnants of the past, the peaty layers read like a gigantic book of prehistory with recognizable pieces like the black bog oaks from the black fen soils, animal remains preserved in oxygen-deprived watery graves and of course the fingerprint of the pollen grain. Believe it or not, many species of plant have a different and distinguishable pollen grain. A core sample through the peat can show which were the dominant trees of bygone eras. The plotting of the progression of vegetation types as climate changed is now a widely-used scientific tool, revealing much about past climatic trends.

Further to the south and east, in the region now called the Broads, a similar but different process was under way. Peats were forming in the estuarine floodplain of a once much larger river system now occupied by the much smaller Bure, Waveney and Yare. Then, the tides of a warmer North Sea ebbed and flowed well inland, making islands out of higher spots like the Suffolk Hundred of Lothingland, now the environs of modern Lowestoft. There is little left of these vast wetlands today, but thanks to the past industry of man there still exist 3,300 hectares – the Norfolk Broads, the most important wetland still remaining in Britain.

The waterlogged layers of peat that lie there today, one above the other, tell us all about the physical and natural history of the Fens during the period of peat formation. The presence of reindeer and creeping willow tell us of the cold spell, at the end of the Ice Time. Representative samples of no less than five of East Anglia's ancient forests have been found in one place, the Isle of Ely, revealing different climatic conditions, spells of warm and cold, wet and dry, which resulted in a continual slow change as conditions dictated the specific make-up of Anglian woodland.

The White Lands

Between modern-day Fenland and the Broads lies the Breckland, an altogether different geological kettle of fish. We include it in our survey of the wetlands of East Anglia at the risk of some hectoring from our scientific colleagues, for the Brecklands is one of the driest parts of Britain, with the lowest rainfall in the country, a historical reputation for rabbit plagues, and a dry desert-like soil that tends to drift like pollen in the wind when exposed to the plough and the air. When compared to the Fens and Broads, the Brecks appear as a hilly and rolling landscape, consisting of stabilized dunes lying on old outcrops of chalk and boulder clay.

But although the wet bits of the Brecklands are few and far between, they are there, and they are important. They consist of a series of meres, or freshwater lakes with some odd features, like

being full of water during a drought, or partly shrunken during a wet period. How did they get there, and what are they?

This has puzzled geomorphologists for years, and a variety of explanations has been put forward, including some fairly fanciful ones. One theory says they are crater holes, formed from displaced meteors falling out of the sky like so much cosmic confetti! The likeliest explanation is less bizarre, but no less interesting, and is fairly logical, given the general pattern of the Breckland landscape.

We know that the area of the Brecklands was once a chalk basin overlain by glacial deposits of sandy, chalky and clay particles. Over time the chalky particles were dissolved and flushed down by percolating rainwater, leaving in many places the dry unstable sand on top. So we ended up with an extraordinary landscape: chalk below and acid sand above, supporting an acid land community of heather, pine and bracken, the predominant vegetation on the dry lands around the meres. The meres then are merely hollows in the glacial sub-soil overlying the chalk, but because of the chalk below, they are filled with alkaline water and support a rich lime-loving vegetation. The hollows themselves may well be kettle holes, formed when ice entombed in the sandy soil eventually melted away. Whichever way they were formed, each

became a lime-rich oasis for plants and animals, set in an acid dune-scape itself set between the lime-rich flowing waters of the Fenlands and the Broads.

When man came to settle in the Brecklands, meres like Ringmere and the Devil's Punchbowl became focal points in the landscape as watering holes for cattle and sources of water supply. The waters, with their rich aquatic vegetation, also became havens for birds passing to and fro between the wetland paradises of the Broads and the Fenland proper. To this day you can still catch the shimmer of white life as swans and gulls fly into the reedy shallows of the white waters overlying the white rock.

Chalk, peat and fen. These are the essential ingredients of East Anglia's unique low landscape, the raw materials which were, in the first instance, shaped by water, but then left in peace by the hand of man. Strange as it may seem, man remains the supreme architect of this wetland wilderness. As we shall discover, we may owe the loss of many wetlands to the actions of man, but the best of the bits that still remain are made, maintained and managed by us.

But first things first. How did the stamp of man first appear on the Anglian scene, and how did those first Anglians behave, each to the other, to keep their heads above the water?

The First Wetlanders

How did the devil come? When first attack?
The church is just the same, though now I know
Fowler of Louth restored it. Time, bring back
The rapturous ignorance of long ago,
The peace, before the dreadful daylight starts
Of unkept promises and broken hearts.

JOHN BETJEMAN, Norfolk

Here Come the Swamp People

During a warm spell between the last two phases of the great
Ice Age something quite remarkable happened: early man.
The first men and women to make their mark on the ancient
icy landscapes of East Anglia belonged to an Old Stone Age
or Paleolithic culture. They ventured across the mudflats and
marshes of the land bridge which connected Britain to Europe,
following in the path of the retreating ice.

This happened over 250,000 years ago. Like many a
broadsman and marshman of later periods, these people lived by
hunting and fishing, making a good living on the abundant
wildlife of the vast wetlands which lay before them.

This pioneering period in Anglian history is known today
as the Hoxnian Interglacial, after the Suffolk village of Hoxne
which lies just south of the river Waveney near Diss. Hoxne
is the site of an ancient lake which formed when the ice
retreated and left a hollow in the boulder clay which covered
the area. Excavations in this old lake have thrown up a
remarkable pollen record which shows how the habitat of the
area changed from Arctic tundra to temperate broadleaf
woodland and then back to tundra.

The men of those days were not like modern man, who did
not appear until 35,000 to 40,000 years ago, but probably
belonged to a race related to Homo Erectus or early
Neanderthal. These people were short and robustly built
with large brow ridges, low sloping foreheads and hardly any
chin.

They were skilled hunters and craftsmen. Beautifully made

flint hand axes and scrapers have been found at Hoxne along with the remains of the animals that the people hunted. Deer, boar, aurochs, elephants and rhinoceros were probably trapped in swamps and killed with clubs and spears. The meat was taken off the bones and prepared for barbecue with the aid of flint knives and scrapers. These people weren't wasteful. The skins of the animals they hunted were used for clothing and the bones put to other uses.

The first Anglians did not, however, like being too cold. When arctic temperatures returned and the land returned to tundra, they moved south in search of the sun.

After their departure, all went quiet. No trace of man has been found for the period when the climate next warmed, 110,000 to 120,000 years ago. There was plenty of game in the form of deer, mammoth, auroch and rhino but apparently no men to hunt them. Wildlife must have flourished during this time and the remains of woolly rhinoceros and mammoth have been found at Homersfield in the Waveney Valley.

Ice was then king for the next 200,000 years or so, until the last cold phase, over 10,000 to 30,000 years ago when ice sheets covered north-west Norfolk and the rest of the area was dominated by tundra and permafrost. But man returned, following the rhinos and mammoths, and it is thought possibly hunting them to extinction. If he, rather than climate and vegetation, is the explanation for their disappearance, then man had made his first of many impacts on the environment of East Anglia.

Stone Free

In time, the climate warmed. The tundra was colonized by silver birch and pine. This in turn gave way to broadleaf woodland of oak and elm. The forests covered everywhere except marshes, river valleys and the coastal fringes. Bands of hunters wandered in and out of East Anglia through the rest of the Palaeolithic and the Mesolithic periods until, with the dawn of Neolithic times, around 6,000 BC, the rising sea level finally severed the continental bridge. Britain had become an island, and, their migrations ended, the first of the island races began to settle down and develop a more sedentary lifestyle of hunting and gathering in the forests and marshes.

They were joined around 6,000 BC by a new wave of immigrants, with a different way of life. These were the Neolithic people, or the people of the New Stone Age. They came to East Anglia not on ague-weakened feet and in the path of migrating deer herds, but by boat. These people came with something else too – agriculture. This was to have an effect on the landscape of East Anglia at the very least comparable to a small Ice Age. For in order to farm, they needed open land for their crops and grazing animals. They started to chop down the trees.

Settlements dating from 6,500 BC to 3,500 BC have been found at Kelling Heath, between Holt and Cromer, and in the Wensum valley. Around 3,500 BC the first true farmers were arriving. Long barrows left by these people have been

located at Ditchingham in the Waveney valley, and at Felthorpe, just north-west of Norwich. It is thought that they worshipped an earth goddess. The long communal burial mounds somehow represented a return to the womb of Mother Earth, and would have been a place of worship.

Possibly these early peoples knew how to respect the earth that gave them a livelihood. But times change, and it is indicative of that change that most of these mounds have long since disappeared from the Anglian flatlands. They have been farmed out of existence. To the south of Norwich at Arminghall, crop marks have shown the site of another place of worship: an early Neolithic temple, or wooden henge. Nothing is visible there now but at one time there stood a horseshoe of massive wooden posts surrounded by a ditch.

The world these people lived, died and worshipped in, though warmer than today's wetlands, was undoubtedly wet. The East Anglian horizon was blanketed with woodland, but the ground was peaty and soft and filled with wetland birds and animals. Towards the coast and the river edges were marshes and reed-beds, fens and meres. Living may have been uncomfortable, a constant battle with biting insects and with sheer unadulterated sogginess, but never was the wildlife so diverse and plentiful, never again was East Anglia so wonderfully wild.

The Neolithic farmers lived in dwellings of stones with ditch fortifications, raising garden crops and grazing animals in the first forest clearings. We know this from prehistoric excavations near Peterborough, and near Maxey, where henges have also been found that date to around 3,300 BC. The ancient Icknield Way connected East Anglia to the monuments at Stonehenge and Avebury in distant Wessex.

Though these ancient wetlanders occupied a wilder wetter environment than their cousins in the west, it is clear that all these people were bound together not just by religion but also by trade, in axes and raw materials. One extraordinary piece of East Anglian prehistory is the monument known as Grimes Graves in the heart of the Brecklands, where flints were mined underground, leaving a complex of shallow potholes spread over a vast area. This lunar landscape still stands today in the heart of Old Anglia, but with some new cousins nearby: one of a number of American airbases.

The Beaker Folk and Queen Boudicca

Then there were the Beaker Folk. The odd name by which we know them had nothing to do with the size of their noses, but with their odd shaped drinking vessels. They were river people, who navigated up the Anglian rivers to reach drier settlements inland. They worshipped a sky god, and buried their dead in barrows, some of which have been found at Ditchingham. And it seemed they were into metal too – bronze in fact – paving the way for a whole new cultural revolution, the Bronze Age.

Bronze Age succeeded Beaker Age around the mid 2,000s BC. The people of the Bronze Age have left their mark here and there on the landscape, in the shape of earthworks and barrows. But the real mark they left upon the land was the large-scale deforestation for agriculture, made possible by their improved tools. What trees these ages left behind were swiftly dealt with by the next of the East Anglian civilizations, the people of the Iron Age, the Iceni, with their splendidly effective metal axes, their magnificent chariots, crafted metalwork jewellery and their horsemanship. Some of their artefacts have remained with us, but they left few hillforts of any significance. Warham Camp is the exception. There are many theories about why this should be, but perhaps the best is ours – they could not find enough hills to put them on.

The Iceni made East Anglia their kingdom. The Gauls who invaded South-East Britain around 75 BC never got as far as Norfolk and the heart of the wetlands. Much mystery surrounds the Iceni empire; we know about them mostly from the later writings of yet another set of invaders of East Anglia, the Romans.

Their own tribal name Ecen may have survived to this day in the place names Ickworth and Icklingham, the word endings suggesting Anglo-Saxon names for Iceni villages or farmsteads. Another echo of the tribe's name lies in the Icknield Way, an ancient track which runs north to south from Snettisham to Thetford.

Horses were highly thought of by the Iceni. The horse motif is repeated time and again on their coins, and has stayed with us today in local language custom. The Norfolk and Lincolnshire word 'ickeny' is used to describe something that is difficult to handle, particularly difficult horses.

Discoveries of coins and jewellery hoards have shown that the Iceni lived all over Norfolk and Suffolk and into the Fens. Sites have been found at Thetford, Bury St Edmunds, King's Lynn, Snettisham and on what had been an island in the Fens where March now stands.

But perhaps the greatest gift of the Iceni to their descendants was a splendid legend, that of Boudicca, a Celtic Mrs Thatcher, who came to prominence in local politics in the early days of the Romans. They first arrived in AD 43, and quickly established themselves in East Anglia as elsewhere in England as the military force to be reckoned with. The Iceni started as allies of the Romans against the common enemy, the Belgae from the south, but in no time at all they became mere client-kings to the Italians. When they tried to assert their independence, and to voice their complaints about the greed of the local Roman priests, the Romans ordered their disarmament. Boudicca, Queen of the proud Iceni, was prepared to take no more.

She marched with a vast army of mighty warriors upon the Roman settlement of Camulodunum, and from there to London, then a small settlement. The city was sacked, the Londoners vanquished, and Queen Boudicca became the toast of the marshlands. Sadly, however, her victory was

Burning straw stubble near Clenchwarton on the Great Ouse Fens.

The mid-summer high spring tides cause thousands
of shoreline birds to flock into Snettisham Reserve
lagoons, among them redshank, oyster-catcher, knot
and occasionally the rare avocet.

Left: Agricultural fenlands on the Holebeach Marshes near Long Sutton.

Right: Lesser swallowtail butterfly.

short-lived. Returning from victory, she was ambushed from behind by the army of Seutonius, Britain's military governor. It was the end of Icenian independence. Boudicca chose death over enslavement, and a dose of poison which she administered herself marked the last act of her Queendom of the Celtic flatlanders.

Romans and Countrymen

By the time the Romans had settled in to East Anglia, an organized agricultural pattern had been established on the land. To this the Romans added new towns, like Cambridge, and built complex canal and drainage schemes to improve the yields of the land. They forced the defeated Celts to build banks along the coast around Lynn to keep out the sea and reclaim the oozy land for agriculture. They built a canal, the Car Dyke, to connect the Cam and the Ouse, and a range of roads converging on Caister, by Norwich.

With the advent of the Romans, the die for England's great wetland wilderness was well and truly cast. For if it was the Stone Age people who first entered the land and the Celts who cleared it, it was the Romans who first drained it and tamed it. The Romans built canals and set in motion the first artificial movement of water around the land, a pattern of water-engineering which was to last for centuries to come.

With the collapse of the Roman administration in AD 407, East Anglia reverted to the control of a range of Celtic tribes,

their Celtic purity re-shaped by the encounter with Rome and with Roman blood. To this hybrid culture the archaeologists gave the term 'Romano-British'.

Suneman's Island

To the meeting of Celt and Roman races others have been added: an assortment of Germanic settlers who came in from the continent, first as mercenaries helping the locals against incursions by Picts and Scots, then as invaders themselves. These were the Angles and the Saxons, and they were responsible for the historic kingdoms of Anglia in Suffolk and Norfolk, and Mercia to the west and north of the Fens. At this time the settlements were mostly confined to small islands in the Fens, as a rising sea level again put low-lying East Anglia under semi-permanent flood conditions.

This may have been the period of the great earthworks, like the Devil's Dyke and the Fleam Dyke. These were not built however against the predations of the sea, but more likely against the predations of the warring Anglian and Mercian tribes, more or less constantly at one another's throats, during the sixth and seventh centuries AD. One such dispute led to the complete sacking of the city of Ely.

Towards the coast, in the flatlands we now know as the Broads, the Saxon Kings held sway over their subjects from small islets, or holms, which lay above the level of the estuarine mud. Most of their subjects must in fact have been the sea and shore birds of this watery wilderness, for the Saxons have left little sign of their historic habitation here. We know of one famous marshman though, the solitary figure of Suneman, who lived a hermit's life on a small oasis he had carved out for himself in the wet heart of the Bure Valley. The Saxons, like the Romans before them, attempted some reclamation from the tidal wastes, this time west of Wisbech.

The history of the wetlands is not complete without reference to the Danes. Year after year during late Roman and Saxon times they ravaged the settlements of the coast and the river valleys. How the locals must have feared the sight of their black war keels and the raven banners flying from the mastheads of their ships. The Vikings took everything they could lay their hands on, including food supplies, ornaments and Saxon women. A couple of atrocities stand out: the sacking of Norwich in 1004 from longships that clearly had no trouble getting up the Bure; and the burning of the Saxon churches in the Waveney valley – filled with local inhabitants. This was their idea of sacrifice – to their merciless war gods Thor and Woden.

Some Vikings however took to the wetlands and settled down, intermarrying with the locals and dividing their time between bouts of rape and pillage and a bit of local fishing. King Canute was one such hybrid. He apparently founded the Abbey of St Bene't at Holm on the same site as had been occupied by Suneman the Saxon hermit. Sadly, no hallmarks of the Danes remain in the old Abbey buildings, but there are Danish endings to some local names, like Rollesby and Mautby.

After the Danes, there came the next set of continental invaders, the Normans, who gave us Norwich Cathedral, a host of local churches and manors, the development of Yarmouth as an international port, and Bungay and Beccles as thriving commercial centres.

Hereward Awake

One East Anglian character was the Saxon lord, Hereward, a sort of Robin Hood of his time. Hereward was apparently away in Flanders when he learned of his father's death and that the Normans, under William the Conqueror, had confiscated his inheritance to give to one of their own vassals.

His anger awoken, he returned hotfoot to his estates at Bourne near Ely and proceeded to drive the dastardly Normans from the place. There he set up a stronghold, together with other dispossessed Saxons. The Isle of Ely was an ideal centre for resistance for two reasons. Firstly it was a kind of Saxon Holy Land, the centre of an area which boasted three famous abbeys: Peterborough, Croyland and Thorney and of course Ely itself. Secondly, it was virtually impenetrable.

Just how impenetrable is illustrated by the writings of one anonymous medieval monk.

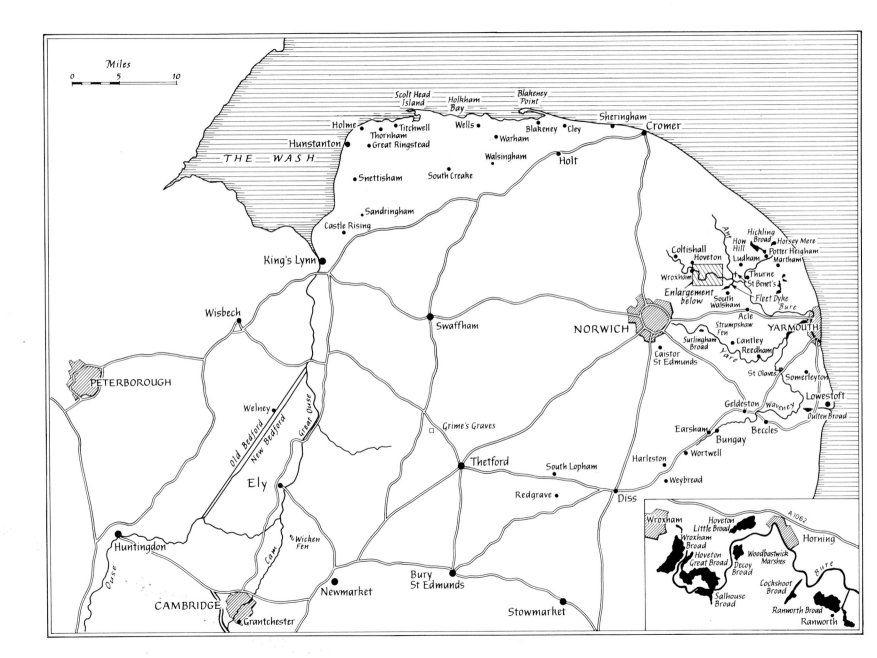

Miles
0   5   10

Scolt Head Island
Holkham Bay
Blakeney Point
Holme
Titchwell
Thornham
Great Ringstead
Wells
Warham
Blakeney
Cley
Sheringham
Cromer
Hunstanton
THE WASH
Walsingham
Holt
Snettisham
South Creake
Sandringham
Castle Rising
Coltishall
How Hill
Hickling Broad
Horsey Mere
Hoveton
Ludham
Potter Heigham
Martham
Wroxham
Thurne
St Benet's
Enlargement below
South Walsham
Fleet Dyke
Bure
King's Lynn
Acle
YARMOUTH
Wisbech
Swaffham
NORWICH
Strumpshaw Fen
Surlingham Broad
Cantley
Reedham
Yare
Caistor St Edmunds
St Olaves
Somerleyton
PETERBOROUGH
Lowestoft
Welney
Geldeston
Waveney
Oulten Broad
Grime's Graves
Earsham
Beccles
Old Bedford
New Bedford
Great Ouse
Bungay
Harleston
Wortwell
Ely
Thetford
South Lopham
Weybread
Wicken Fen
Redgrave
Diss
Cam
Huntingdon
Ouse
CAMBRIDGE
Newmarket
Bury St Edmunds
Stowmarket
Grantchester

Wroxham
Hoveton Little Broad
A 1062
Wroxham Broad
Hoveton Great Broad
Decoy Broad
Woodbastwick Marshes
Horning
Cockshoot Broad
Bure
Salhouse Broad
Ranworth Broad
Ranworth

over into the specially created strip of flood plain between the two.

When the flood subsided, water was released by means of a sluice into the lower reaches of the New Bedford River, or the Hundred Foot Drain as it was known because it was 100 feet wide. The Hundred Foot Drain was a major engineering project. Five hundred Scottish prisoners and 1,000 Dutch 'navigators' (hence the word 'navvies') were employed in the back-breaking work.

Today, the drainage system remains almost the same. When the Ouse reaches flood level, a sluice gate is opened at Earith allowing the water to rush into the Old Bedford River. The water spills into the flood plain between the two rivers, known as the Ouse Washes. On a number of occasions, the flooding has lasted for up to three weeks, and it is a pattern that can be repeated three to four times every winter. Flooding is rarer, but not unheard of, during the summer months when it causes damage to hay crops and nests.

As the winter floods recede, the pools of shallow water which linger on the sodden pasture create ideal sites for wildfowl and waders. Being relatively inaccessible and uncultivated, the Ouse Washes are a haven for wetland birds; indeed the Washes have been designated as one of the UK's forty Ramsar sites because they are home to internationally important numbers of waders and waterfowl.

Perhaps the best illustration of the impact on fenland landscape by the actions of the drainage enthusiasts can be seen from what was lost at Whittlesey Mere after it was drained in 1851.

The Water varied in depth from two to five feet, and was surrounded by reed-shoal, which formed a beautiful and valuable fringe. The reeds extended over an area of 200 acres, and yielded annually about a thousand bundles, valued at a pound apiece . . . Over the reed shoal hovered myriads of insects, including the majestic Swallow Tail (*Papilio machaon*) and the brilliant Large Copper (*Polyommatus dispar*), both of which have long since vanished from the scene, the latter, indeed having become extinct.

SAMUEL MILLER AND SYDNEY SKETCHLY, *The Fenland, Past and Present*

The mere, a substantial body of water 2½ miles long and occupying an area of 1,000 to 1,600 acres, was also a favourite place for local boating and fishing and for skating in the winter. But after drainage was completed there was nothing left, not even a little damp corner for some sparrow to bathe in. Where coot and moorhen once swam, now rich fields of monocrop corn waved across the landscape.

Fenland history is not complete without mention of windmills. As the area was drained, the peat shrank and the level of the fields fell, making it essential to pump the water out of the ditches. The succession story is the same as in the Broads – first windpumps, then steam, and finally diesel and electric pumps have taken over. That's a story, however, for another place.

Wetland Worlds

How cold the bathe, how chattering cold the drying
  How welcoming the inland reeds appear
The wood-smoke and the breakfast and the frying
  And your warm freshwater ripples, Horsey Mere.

JOHN BETJEMAN, *East Anglian Bathe*

Wetland Wonderland

Wetlands mean a multitude of different things to different
people. To the boating crowd, a wetland is a vast stretch of
open water where they can tussle with the wind. For the reed
cutter and thatcher, a wetland is a source of raw material, a
source of income. To the farmer, it is a series of decisions
about dyke levels, drainage and grazing, and to the bird watcher
and botanist the value of the wetlands lies in the diversity of
the landscape and its biology, from the mudflats and salt
marshes of the Wash and North Norfolk coast, through to the
reed-bed, fen, carr and oak woodland of the Broads, and the
meres of Breckland.

Wetlands for all Seasons

Forget the clichés about the sap rising and new life stirring; the
first days of spring on the wetlands can be bleak. Vast
expanses of flooded grazing marches stretch to the horizon,
topped by a sky which threatens more icy drizzle and
knuckle-freezing winds. But such bleak landscapes have their
own beauty and sense of exhilaration when you think you are
the only one foolhardy enough to venture forth.

There is hope on the horizon. The first avocets arrive at their
favourite haunts in March; the terns return from their winter
travels and the first chiffchaff can be heard singing from the
top of its alder tree perch. There is hope in the form of more
temperate days when the sun warms the air, giving a tantalizing
taste of what is to come. The woodland birds are now in full
song; the ducks and waders are showing off their plumage to
attract a mate, the brown reeds contrast starkly with the clear
cold black water of the rivers and pools.

Wherry Hathor *at Reedham on the River Yare.*

By April the bittern is booming and the marsh harriers are in full display flight. The people's naturalist Ted Ellis, ever a sensitive observer of the seasons, reflected on the awakening of April in 1972:

The wakening of April has begun to coax life from the winter-brown marshes very swiftly in the past week, and even reluctant reed-colts are now shooting up like smooth asparagus in the stubbles surrounded by the splendour of marsh marigolds . . . In shadowy swamps there are verdant clumps of water forget-me-nots, neat, blue-green tufts of sedge and the lengthening sword leaves of irises.

TED ELLIS, *Countryside Reflections*

By May there is a sense of release. Blossoms brighten the hedgerows, cow parsley walks tall in the meadows, yellow flag, with its stiff, sword-like leaves and yellow flower, glows in the meadows and the water violet blooms in the dykes. And let's not forget that other species which is a good-time visitor to its favourite habitat – the common tourist who begins to put in an appearance in his holiday plumage about this time. The cafés scrub down their plastic tables and chairs, the pub trade picks up, and cruisers take to the water again – the season has begun.

Discover the quiet wetland corners in summer, and you'll uncover an era we all believed had gone. A time when butterflies flit from plant to plant; dragonflies deftly skim the water surface and the air fills with the sweet noise of birdsong. The beautiful swallowtail butterfly is out on its travels – a strident flash of yellow and black fleeting across the fen. The sedge is cut, the hay is mown, although careful conservationists take care to check the beds for wildlife first so as not to carve up important insects' or birds' nests.

Plants which have slept below the surface in the dykes and open water put in a brief appearance; water soldier thrusts its white flower into the sunshine and the cool white waterlily reveals itself for summer.

It is the time for birds to raise their young: the rare little terns which raise fledglings on some areas of beach; in the reeds, if your eyes are sharp, you might catch sight of a bearded tit, Cetti's warbler, reed, sedge and grasshopper warblers

feeding on rich insect populations. Cast your eyes higher and
you might be lucky enough to see a heron roost, and then
look low over the fields and marshes for the slow wing beat
of the marsh harrier as it glides towards its ground-level nest.

But there is another side to summer. The rivers of Broadland
teem with cruisers, leaving in their wake a perpetual stream
of wash relentlessly pounding the fragile banks. Litter is
dropped; lead fishing weights, now frowned upon, once
poisoned many birds; and the detritus that follows man
everywhere floats between the banks or sinks to the bottom to
puzzle the archaeologists of the future – if our global detritus
allows us a future! Even the noble swans beg for food from the
tourists. Under the weight of such undignified commercial
pressure the beauty of the area begins to pall.

Autumn is a time to re-group. The swifts and swallows
show us the way, lining up like soldiers along the telegraph
wires, seemingly for miles on end, waiting to leave. Look out
at dawn in November and you might see the lingering wisps
of mist just hanging over the marshes. The mist dissolves and
the day evolves into unlooked-for warming sunshine. The
reds, browns, yellows are echoed in the water and the
surrounding fields saturated with dew.

But the whole cycle culminates in winter when the
over-wintering flocks of pintail, mallard and widgeon congregate
on the stretches of mudflats at Breydon Water, Yarmouth, at
Titchwell and Snettisham on the Wash. Thousands of little
knot can be counted. Bewick's swan, the least common British

swan, is a winter visitor, and even the rare ruff can be seen.

When the tide goes out on the mudflats the herons might arrive to spear some prey. The chunky oystercatcher makes his noisy presence felt, the curlew, redshank, snipe and dunlin all forage in the mud and over everything looms the ominous presence of the cormorant, perching on channel markers, as it dolefully hangs out its black wings to dry.

Move inland a little and you will witness a hive of activity. The reed cutter stands knee-deep in icy water, his scythe slicing rhythmically through the tall reeds. For the months of winter are when the fruits of the reed-beds are harvested. When the elements are at their most vindictive, this tough breed brave the raw east wind to bring in the crop.

They don't wear gloves, so at first their hands get torn to ribbons by the sharp-edged reeds and chapped by the cold. Gradually the skin hardens and the callouses appear. The reed stands in water and must be cut four inches below the surface. Old hands reckon it's something that can't be taught; it's an art – some can cut reed, some can't.

Watching a reed cutter at work is mesmerizing; his scythe, moulded to his style and shape, slices through reed after reed: all felled at a stroke. After a while, the cutter pauses, straightens his back and leans on his scythe for a breather. Look at his nails: they are probably worn down by the abrasiveness of the reeds. Jackets and clothes get torn as they catch on the bundles and the spiteful reeds strike back by cutting face and hands.

Once cut, the reed must be bundled. It is collected by the

Marshman Eric Edwards with sedge at How Hill (opposite).

Eric reed dressing in front of an audience (below).

armful, raked into shape, thumped on the ground, tied up and the size checked by measuring 'three hands and a bit' around its girth. Traditionally the bundles would have been carried shoulder high to a flat-bottomed reed boat and transported along the dyke system to the river bank. But technology, in the form of an amphibious craft which skims across cut reed-beds and water alike, carrying as many as seventy bundles, has made a welcome appearance in some places.

While some reed is still harvested by hand, most is now cut by a machine which is pushed through the reed-beds like an old-fashioned plough. It cuts and ties the reed in rough bundles which then have to be re-tied, usually in a chilly shed near the water's edge. As the harvest progresses, sometimes over as long as three months, a satisfying mound of bundled reeds begins to grow, piled so neatly and uniformly you could almost believe they had been cut with a guillotine.

Many believe that for beauty alone, the wetlands are unrivalled in winter. There is that curious stillness, interrupted by the hissing reeds; the golden brown of the reed fringing the water's edge which in turn reflects and refracts the winter light of East Anglia's big skies.

Here Come the Trees

From one point of view, the open water of the wetland could be seen as a frustrated woodland.

The reed fringe of the average Norfolk Broad is forever

trying to advance, constantly seeking to engulf the water in a carpet of reed. The swaying heads of reed are a classic feature of the Broadland scene. But mile upon relentless mile of reeds, whatever its visual charm, was once part of an old Broadland monoculture.

The beds bore rich fruit for man, giving him reed for roofs, sedge for the ridge of a thatch, fodder and litter for cattle, all of which were transported by river on an elaborate system of dykes. But left unharvested the reeds sow the seeds of their own demise. Dead and decaying reeds begin to pile up around the new growth, and over the years, the reed-bed begins to dry out. Little by little, other plants begin to creep in from the margins and as they do, they add their own burdens of dead and decaying vegetation, until eventually, the character of the bed is transformed from a monoculture to a mixed ecology of plants, forming a marsh. Over time, the marsh begins to suffer from the same excesses as the reed-bed; abundant growth leads to an abundance of organic detritus and the roots have to dig even deeper for life-giving moisture. Slowly trees and shrubs begin to encroach; willow and alder carr take a hold and the long process of succession to oak woodland begins.

Without the farming methods of fifty or more years ago, which meant regular cutting and managing of these Fenland areas – an ecological restraining order if you like – it is inevitable they disappear. With them go marshland plants and animals.

Alder carr is perhaps the nearest we get to a tropical swamp. The ground is boggy, often giving off a rich and foetid smell.

Instead of a light, airy fen where the butterflies flit and the dragonflies hover, there is a tangled web of woodland. It is not that this is without its wildlife interest; the trees and shrubs provide shelter for birds and shade-tolerant plants stand a chance of competing successfully.

Indeed a mix of alder carr, marsh, fen and reed-bed can provide one of the most interesting and diverse ecological communities, a range of habitats that many reserve wardens seek to emulate.

But slowly the open water and reed-beds have declined. Over the last fifty years the transformation from fen to woodland has proceeded more rapidly as the demand for fen products like thatch has declined. Currently there is a resurgence of interest in reed as a thatching material, but this has come late in the day and now many once-productive beds are no more, and of course the passage of time has reduced the thatching workforce. If you like the trees, this may not be a bad thing, but there is a loss in diversity, which it is perhaps desirable to correct.

Part of that natural wetland diversity is of course made up of the little cousins to the trees: the wetland grasses, sedges and herbs. Plants may not be as exciting as birds or as awe-inspiring as other members of the animal kingdom, but their part in the chain of life is fundamental. From the expanses of reeds to the isolated fen orchid and from the sturdy trees to delicate water weeds, the threats to our native plants have never been greater. And predictably man has played his traditional role

Turn, turne and Thurne again: a windmill on the River Thurne.

in this depressing scenario. Pollution, land drainage, and habitat loss take their toll.

At the time when P. H. Emerson was taking his evocative photographs of the Broads nearly a century ago, the water was crystal clear and a carpet of waterlilies rested gracefully on the surface, as a diversity of insects flitted from plant to plant. The banks were gently sloping, allowing different species to get a foothold; sewage effluent was not pumped routinely into the river system and less nitrate drained from surrounding fields. It all gave plants the chance to survive and they in turn provided havens for insects which fed the fish, which in turn fed the heron and the harrier. But many of the plants once common on the Broads, gems like the water soldier, cowbane, marsh pea and the marsh sow thistle are now rarities.

The same is true of the surrounding fen where the fen orchid and the narrow buckler fern were once commonplace. Thankfully the milk parsley, on which the spectacular swallowtail butterfly caterpillar feeds, has secured a stronghold in places like How Hill as a result of the action of conservationists.

The Broads have their share of animal oddities too. The fen raft spider, a veritable giant of the arachnid world – it is bigger than a child's outstretched hand – is restricted to reed- and weed-filled ponds and dykes. The Norfolk aeshna, one of the country's rarest dragonflies, is currently the recipient of much local conservation interest as attempts are made to protect the last vestige of its habitat. Both are protected under the Wildlife and Countryside Act, but what good is the protection if their homes are drained, ploughed and polluted?

Hickling and its Guardian

The seasonal cycle of the wetlands was once the essence of life in East Anglia. It was all around and no one took much notice of it. Now we rely on nature reserves and conservation bodies to maintain what has become precious. East Anglia is rich in nature reserves, from the vast tracts of coastal mudflats in the north to the wetlands of the Broads and the open marshes of the Fens. Two of the most important are Hickling Broad and Wicken Fen.

Hickling is vast, over 1,308 acres, with the largest stretch of open water in Broadland. It has international status as part of the Hickling-Horsey-Martham Ramsar Convention site; it is home to large numbers of wintering wildfowl; visited by many waders and summer visitors include Cetti's warblers, common and little terns. Beautiful, wild and teeming with wildlife, Hickling is also beloved by the tourists, particularly the wind-surfers. In protecting his empire, the warden, Francis Russell, has a delicate task to perform. He needs the knowledge of a countryman, the scientific insight of a botanist, the tact of a diplomat and the financial skills of a businessman.

He works shoulder-to-shoulder with men who have been working the marshes all their lives. He is also the PR man dealing with the public, and giving talks to visitors; and he has

to enter the world of commerce, finding buyers for the annual £14,000 crop of reed and sedge the reserve markets.

Unlike many of the lower profile reserves, Hickling is blessed with a number of sources of income – reed, sedge, grazing rights, eel and fishing permits, rents from moorings, income from permits to visit the reserve, the water-trail boat trips, and grants from the Nature Conservancy Council.

Francis decides how much reed will be cut each season. He also has to make often crucial decisions about machinery. Does he keep the old machine going with a few new sprockets and belts or does he commit the Norfolk Naturalists' Trust, which owns the reserve, to investing in a brand new £8,000 machine?

He is not romantic about the old ways of doing things. He is quite prepared to borrow crawler tractors from kindly farmer neighbours to drag the reed from the reed-bed when, years ago, the cutters would have put it on their backs and taken it to boats. As he says, 'Those days are gone, it's history now. You've got to be a bit more mechanical.'

The total budget for Hickling in a year is about £64,000 which is a big responsibility for anyone without business training. So does Francis feel he was adequately trained for what could be seen as a manager's job? 'I trained myself in a way. I was self-employed for eighteen months and I kept my own books so I had a shrewd idea about making things balance. It is an aspect of the job that I really didn't appreciate – I don't think you do until you take over,' he said.

After the dearth of visitors to Hickling in winter, the spring brings them all out. 'It's really quite a pleasant relief to see people again. Four months of being stuck on a reed-bed with just a few faces for company, it is a welcome change.' But he adds, 'By the end of the summer, I'm glad they're going away, not because I'm anti-social, but because I like to have time to myself and have a bit of a break.'

There are wardens who give the impression that they tolerate the presence of the public under protest, looking on them as little more than irritating visitors in their back garden. Francis however sees himself much more in the role of guardian. 'I happen to be fortunate enough to be given the chance to look after it for others. That doesn't mean I don't care about the place, but hopefully I don't feel that possessive.'

For Francis, Hickling is more than just a place, it is an experience. 'To try and describe the magic of Hickling is like trying to describe the beauty of one of Leonardo's paintings.' He revels in its dynamism – one moment serene and calm, the next turbulent and unpredictable. He loves the winter light and the cacophony of sounds from birds, insects, trees and water. But above all, it is a solid, reliable, dependable place with a history and, hopefully, a continuity – something that too much of the English countryside lacks.

'I care about looking after Hickling but it's not enough. It's no use being short sighted when the rest of the country is becoming a mass of roads and little suburban belts of lots of smart twee bungalows. I am in the job because I care about the wildlife and the countryside in Norfolk. I feel strongly about Norfolk. I care about the way it's changing and about the things that are here and I enjoy its beauty and the magic of certain places, particularly the Broads.'

Preserving Wicken

Wicken Fen in the heart of the Fen country is the jewel in the crown of Fenland conservation, saved by the Victorians as a collectors' piece from the predations of the Fenland drainers.

The entomologists had already lost another precious site, Whittlesey Mere, to the march of agricultural improvement and they were determined Wicken should not go the same way. So they set about buying it and giving it piecemeal to the National Trust, not through any deep-seated desire to conserve it, but rather to preserve it as their favourite collecting playground.

So in 1899 Wicken became Britain's first-ever nature reserve. It was a close shave. Those responsible for draining the Fens had Wicken next on their list, but the locals who relied on its Fenland harvest for a living put up such a strong fight that part of what is now the nature reserve remained virgin fen, unaffected by the mechanics of drainage.

Today Wicken is a curious mix. Sedge Fen, the area nearest to the village, has never been drained and so is a naturalist's paradise. The other main area is Adventurers' Fen which was drained, and because, as a result, it houses fewer wetland plant species, it is less important from a botanical point of view. Here the Trust has artificially turned back the clock and re-dug an area of open water.

It is ironical that Sedge Fen, which has never been drained, is now the driest area on the reserve. The reason is that drainage caused the peat of the surrounding fen to shrink, leaving Sedge Fen high and dry as an island.

Wicken Fen's establishment as a nature reserve meant little at the time. Nature conservation and management as we know it today had never been thought of, and the fen was allowed to deteriorate. Without the regular regime of sedge cutting and litter harvesting which the local fenfolk had practised, the choking encroachment of scrubland quickly took a hold. If later naturalists had not seen what was happening, Wicken Fen today could be oak woodland.

Since the 1950s, a massive clearance programme has been undertaken to remove the invading scrub and re-establish a pattern of management which reflects the traditional regime of the fen. Sedge is regularly harvested and sold though not as much as in days gone by. In the past, the Cambridge colleges bought vast quantities for tinder, and there was a sedge merchant in Wicken village until 1900.

Milk parsley, the food of the swallowtail butterfly caterpillar, once thrived on the Fen. Today none of these striking creatures is to be found here, but the Trust believes it stands a good chance of re-introducing the butterfly in the near future.

Litter was traditionally cut for hay in the last century and was used as a covering for the floors of Newmarket's racing stables. Today litter is still cut because it maintains such a rich wildlife habitat, but the crop is no longer in demand and instead is gathered and burnt.

Walk round Wicken Fen and you could be treading on a 300-year-old drove, a wide pathway originally used by those working on Sedge Fen. Today these wide straight tracks, teaming with fascinating vegetation, beckon invitingly, criss-crossing the Fen in a maze of parallel lines.

It's easy to get lost at Wicken, not in the conventional sense, but lost in history, treading the paths that fen countrymen and women once trod, not for pleasure, but to survive; to cut their

sedge for roofs, dig their peat for fuel and shoot the birds for food. Today the harvest is a different one: scientific knowledge, and the pleasure of once again seeing plants like ragged robin, purple loosestrife and yellow flag flourish while all around the thick black soil yields standard vegetables.

Broadlands for the Birds

Explore Ranworth and you are exploring a Broadland microcosm. Open water, reed-beds, alder carr and fen are all jostling for space, while the birds wheel and dive, battling for the best nesting and feeding sites, free from the intrusion of the boating fraternity. Ranworth Broad is closed to navigation. The birds, fish, insects and plantlife have the whole stretch of open water to themselves, under the protection of the Norfolk Naturalists' Trust which owns the Broad and surrounding Fen.

Once famed wildfowling territory, Ranworth and Cockshoot Broads were handed over in 1949 by their owner Colonel Henry Cator. He gave the Trust a prime site in the heart of Broadland, a site which has become a key weapon in getting the conservation message across.

A boardwalk has been laid from the village, which passes through oak wood, jungle-like swamp of alder carr, reed-beds and finally leads to open water, overlooked by the Broadland Floating Conservation Centre, a unique thatched building moored in the water on floating pontoons.

Great crested grebes, coots, swans and ducks all nest on the Broad, and in summer common terns breed on rafts specially put there for them. The Broad itself suffers from pollution like the rest of the area and the Trust fights a perpetual battle to restore the reed fringe which provides nesting sites.

But the water is only half the story. At the far end of the Broad lies the series of interconnecting dykes, weaving their way through acres of unreclaimed fen which make up part of the Bure National Nature Reserve, one of the most important centres for wetland conservation in Britain.

It is rich in plant life and is home to the swallowtail butterfly. With volunteer help, the Trust is gradually clearing all the dykes and eventually hopes to connect the system with neighbouring Cockshoot Broad. The sedge from Ranworth is said to be highly sought after by thatchers who can recognize it by its smell; before it is mowed, all the swallowtail caterpillars are removed to safety.

Halvergate Marshes is the biggest complex of its kind in the country. In earlier times the marshes would flood in winter and provide ideal shallow conditions for overwintering and breeding wetland birds, but when the efficient electric pump was introduced, drainage became feasible and the pattern of farming changed from summer grazing to arable crops.

Some of the marshes are part of the RSPB's Berney Marshes Nature Reserve. Dams and sluices have been built to maintain shallow flooding for winter and spring birds. Widgeon, pintail, teal, shoveler, gadwall, Bewick swans, geese and waders use the pools in winter and in spring the damp grassland is a haven for redshank, lapwing, mallard, shoveler and gadwall.

In summer sheep and cattle peacefully graze, stretching as far as the eye can see, the horizon only punctured by the odd derelict windmill or delapidated farm building.

The Last Refuges: Welney and Cley

Naturalist and painter Sir Peter Scott first visited the Ouse Washes in 1928. It was a visit which was to spark off an interest in wildfowl and eventually lead to the establishment of the Wildfowl Trust, with its aims of conservation, education, research and recreation.

The Trust's site at Welney in the Fens was set up by Sir Peter Scott as an inviolate sanctuary for the birds which live in and pass through the Fens every year, a place where water birds could exist in peace. And yet, through careful planning, the Trust has managed to let the public enjoy the spectacle without destroying the essential wildness of the Ouse Washes, now an internationally important wetland.

Bewick's swans, each with their unique beak markings, are a major success story of Welney. Before the refuge was set up, as few as thirty of these stately birds wintered on the Washes. Now over 2,000 are not an uncommon sight. And what a sight! During the day the swans feed on surrounding farmland, but at dusk they come home to Welney to roost, wheeling in across the Fens, providing a thrilling and awe-inspiring spectacle. There they are fed daily – only a small amount, enough to whet their appetites, not satisfy them.

Whooper swans also winter at Welney, and a large number of mute swans live and nest on the Washes. Literally thousands of ducks winter on the refuge – widgeon, mallard, teal, pochard, pintail, shoveler, tufted and gadwall. When they're all in full cry, the noise is deafening. Other birds include flocks of black-headed gulls and small gaggles of geese. Short-eared owls and cormorants are regular winter visitors and marsh harriers visit in summer and autumn.

The character of the refuge changes in summer when the foreign visitors have gone away. Black-tailed godwits and ruffs now breed on the refuge in summer. They were once common breeding birds before large-scale drainage of the Fens; in the late eighteenth century godwits would be fattened up by local fenmen and sold for as much as five shillings (25p) each because of their tasty meat.

Over 260 species of flowering plants have been recorded here, and the ditches are rich in aquatic plants. Providing the flooding has subsided, it is possible in summer to walk across the Washes. It is a chance to savour the Fen countryside at its best; to take in its sounds and marvel at its low horizon and never-ending sky.

To the success stories of Hickling and Welney must be added that of Cley Marshes on the North Norfolk coast. With its fresh and saltwater marshes, grazing marshes, scrapes and shingle bank, Cley is an exceptional place for birds, with an exceptional history.

In 1926, 407 acres at Cley came up for auction. They were bought by a group of enlightened ornithologists, who preferred at the time to remain anonymous, for the sum of £5,160, 'with the object,' they said, 'of preserving this property as a bird-breeding sanctuary for all time'.

But the anonymous ornithologists were actually to achieve much more. Soon after they had bought the marshes they met in the George Hotel at Cley and decided it should be handed over to a trust to be managed as a bird-breeding sanctuary. And so the Norfolk Naturalists' Trust was born – the first county wildlife trust, and Cley Marshes became the first county reserve in Britain.

The Founders of the Trust were sufficiently forward thinking to write at the time:

When one considers the changes in the face of the county that are being made or are being contemplated by Forestry Commissioners, Drainage Boards, speculative builders and the like, one is anxious to preserve for future generations areas of marsh, heath, woods, undrained fenland, with the natural wealth of fauna and flora. At the present time most of Broadland is in the hands of owners who can be relied upon not to interfere with the natural beauties of the district, but who shall say what will happen in a hundred or even ten years' time!

But there were still engrained traditions to be observed. The winter duck shooting rights were let to help bring in some income. This was justified on the grounds that overseas birds came in such numbers and did not breed at Cley so they were considered 'legitimate game for the wildfowler, and are, by the way, excellent eating'.

For as long as the reserve has been open to excite and inspire visitors, a member of the Bishop family has been its guardian. Gamekeeper on the reserve in 1926 was Robert Bishop, great grandfather of the present warden, Bernard. Bernard's father, Billy, took over in 1939.

Billy Bishop was warden for forty-two years. 'He was really the person who changed it; he originally made the scrapes, or shallow lagoons favoured by wading birds. During his forty-two years he saw a marvellous amount of change. In the early days everybody came and then shot everything and then the transformation came and people used to come with binoculars and notebooks, and nowadays they bring telescopes,' said Bernard.

But Billy Bishop could never be called a bird watcher. 'He was a countryman. He knew all about the weather, he was really a true countryman, and a naturalist as well which is more important. Anybody can learn birds; anybody can sit down and study birds, but it's knowing how to get birds to where you want them and then how to keep them there and how to manage the land that's important,' said Bernard.

He recalls how in the early days before the visitors' centre was built, the bird watchers would congregate on a Sunday morning in an old wooden hide. 'It was the gathering place; Father had probably been to the football at Norwich on the Saturday and there was always a discussion about the game.

'I remember one Sunday when we were there, this young chap came in and said to Father: "Is there much about? Is it worth me buying a permit?"

'Well I cringed up in the corner because I knew what Father would think and he really tore into the man. The one thing he used to get very irate about was the younger generation coming in – the twitcher type of people.'

Bernard, like his father, is a practical man. 'I'm not the sort of person who can sit in a hide and watch birds all day, but I could spend a day messing round with the water levels,' he said.

When Bernard left school he spent a few years bait digging and cutting reed in the winter. He then worked for a local plumber, but hated every minute of the work. All the while he was helping his father, watching what he did, learning from him, and for a while worked alongside him as summer warden. When Billy retired in 1979, it was part of the natural succession for Bernard to take over.

Not surprisingly, he feels a close affinity with the reserve. 'I feel as though it's mine.' But you sense a certain unease about the future. Ask him if another Bishop son will take over when he retires and Bernard shakes his head and says: 'I don't know. They look towards people who've got degrees and God knows what today.'

But just as the natural sciences would have been all the poorer without the input of 'amateurs and enthusiasts' such as Darwin among others, so too the world of conservation would suffer a great loss if the likes of the Bishops were no longer to be found treading the boardwalks of reserves like Cley. With the experience and the insight that comes from practical work and from previous generations, they are the natural guardians of the world of nature. Long may the reign of the Bishops last over the Marshes of Cley.

Return of the Bittern

Booming Marvellous

Every place of distinction has its magic beast, its totem animal or bird. The North Pennines and the Tower of London have their ravens, America has its bald eagle, Scotland its golden eagle. When these totems go, according to tradition, so also something else passes by: a freedom; a wilderness; a piece of the ecological web that binds everything.

Similarly, East Anglia has its magic beast: the bittern. The natural habitat of this solitary bird is reed-bed, silent reeds, away from people, away from predators, away from pressure, somewhere it can boom, and in that hollow boom echo both the sound and the ancient damp silences of the marshes. Time was when the bittern fled its wetland world; and no boom echoed across the marshes. But the story did not end there.

It is often said in Broadland that if the distinctive boom of the male bittern is heard, then all is right with Broadland. If a season passes without its mating call, the naturalists are understandably uneasy. Not that the bittern is often seen, for its shy nature and its camouflage make it a rare and elusive quarry for the binocular brigade.

With its long pointed bill thrust straight up, bright eyes half-closed, the feathers of head and neck smoothed downwards so that their alternate dark and light markings blend with the reeds, the bird just melts into the background. It is even said to sway gently with the reeds. Its big green legs and feet, partially submerged in water, can easily be taken for reed-stalks.

During the early eighteenth century there were bitterns in abundance on the Broads and in the Fens, particularly Wicken Fen. Naturalists recorded that it was possible to see four or five in a morning. But no one counted on the impact of the then predations of man. It was not unknown for fen shooters to bag twenty or thirty in a morning, and it made a popular Sunday midday meal among fenfolk of the time. Ten thousand bittern dinners later, and by the mid 1850s the bittern became

extinct as a breeding species. Would-be residents did not get much of a chance. During the next sixteen years, over 100 continental immigrants were shot in Norfolk. The bittern abandoned East Anglia and retired to safer reed-beds overseas.

But quite out of the blue, in 1911, ornithological history was made when a half-fledged bittern was discovered at Sutton Broad. Then, in 1917, Hickling became colonized, probably due to the fact that many of the guns were away fighting in the fields of Flanders. In 1928, twenty-five boomers were recorded and by the 1930s the breeding area had extended into North Norfolk. They reached a population peak in the '50s with about sixty booming males making their presence known by 1954. But this success was not to last.

Bird numbers went into steep decline, and then crash. Cold winters, water pollution from the new intensive farming, habitat loss and increased disturbance all proved bad news for the boomer. By the 1970s the county total was reduced to twenty-eight boomers. By 1976, there were only nine left in the whole Broads area. By 1989 only three boomers were reported in the whole of Broadland. Now, you may be lucky enough to hear one. The boom is repeated only three or four times in a day or night, and then only in the months of April and May. If your hearing is exceptional, or if you're very close, listen out for the coughs and clicks as it breathes in for the big boom.

One naturalist who made a reputation for herself on the back of a boom was Emma Louise Turner, author of an early natural history of the Broads published in 1924. She records a chance sighting with a Broadsman helper of the mysterious bittern on 8 July 1911. She records 'The never-to-be-forgotten July 8th was a terribly hot day, and I cannot say that either of us felt particularly hopeful as we climbed through the ridge of an old boathouse at 2pm, armed with newspapers to protect the backs of our necks from the blazing sun.'

But after forty-five minutes they were rewarded. 'In the brilliant sunshine and against a background of green trees the bird appeared to be a bright cinnamon brown; her slow flapping flight resembled that of a short-eared owl, while in shape she was like a heron.'

After several hours' vigilance from the uncomfortable vantage point of an alder tree, followed by a sweeping search, knee-deep in watery reed-bed, they finally found one of the youngsters.

'How we gloated over our prize as he stood there transformed into the resemblance of a bunch of reeds!' At 3 a.m. the next morning they were off again to retrieve the bittern from where they had safely stowed him for the night and to return the youngster to its habitat. 'When I put him on the ground he stalked off in a solemn and what was intended to be a dignified manner. In reality he appeared very ludicrous; for with big green legs and splayed feet, drooping wings and head held high in the air, he looked like a tall, gaunt old woman masquerading in bird's attire.'

Seven years later Miss Turner was to see her first young

bittern in the nest. She described it thus: 'The young bittern was the quaintest little ornithological oddity I had ever seen; he looked more like a small animated golliwog than anything else.'

Catch that Coypu

If being bitten by the bittern bug is one extreme of wetland natural history, being bitten by coypus is the other. Sighting an indigenous wetland species like a bittern may be a rare event these days, but an even rarer event would be to catch sight of a coypu. In fact it would not happen. There are no coypus in East Anglia, but this was not always so.

The coypu is a funny-looking rodent with huge carrot-coloured front teeth, endearing in its way. It is South American in origin. It was introduced in the 1930s to satisfy the demand for 'nutria', a fashionable fur at the time. The fur farms however were ramshackle affairs and many animals escaped. The coypu went native, and in East Anglia it found itself truly at home.

Coypus are big animals, weighing up to 18 lbs each, and their impact on the Anglian scene was correspondingly large. In the wetlands they found a habitat similar to their native swamps. The escapees bred successfully and started to do serious damage. Not content merely with tunnelling into the banks of ditches and rivers, they ate their way through local crops including sugar beet, brassicas and cereals. They also

tucked in to a wide range of native wetland plants including the flowering rush and cowbane.

Worse still, coypus devastated large areas of the reed swamp that ringed many of the broads and rivers. Some countrymen will tell how their dykes had never been clearer and cleaner than when the coypus were around to eat all the encroaching vegetation. But on the whole their activities threatened to undermine the balance of the entire wetland ecology. This was made worse by the fact that the breeding habits of the coypu are comparable to those of the rabbit.

By the late 1950s the coypu population had reached a

maximum of about 200,000. The effects of their insatiable appetite were beginning to tell. In October 1960 entire osier beds were destroyed at Burgh Castle; even tough osier whips could not compete with the big teeth of these funny furry beasts. Coypus would bend the osier canes to get at the tasty new shoots. Many canes were left broken or so bent they became useless for the basketware business. The coypus even went for sedge on the Norfolk Naturalists' Trust reserve at Hickling.

Officialdom moved in to stop the march of the coypu. In 1962 the Ministry of Agriculture launched a three-year campaign to trap the animals. Their initial efforts devastated the population, and by 1965 there were about 5,000 left. The decline however proved to be a temporary hiccup and by 1975 the coypus were back on top, with a population of about 19,000.

The Ministry launched a research programme called Coypu Control to see how the coypu could be controlled in the most efficient way, and it hired a team of trappers to implement the eradication. At first the coypus resisted the new attack and continued to wreak havoc in the wetlands.

By 1980, Coypu Control grew to meet the furry menace. A budget of £2.5 million and a team of three chief coypu persons and twenty-four trappers was unleashed on the Broads. The trappers stood to win a bonus of three times their annual salary if they wiped out the coypus within a fixed period of six years. The luckless creatures were lured into cages on floating rafts using carrots as bait. It meant trappers could free the moorhens, coots, ducks and even the odd heron, but for the coypu it was a swift death at the hands of a .22 target pistol.

At the start of April 1981 there were more than 5,000 adult coypu in the wetlands. By April 1986 there were fewer than forty. Now the problem was switched to finding the last survivors. Could Coypu Control ever be really sure they'd all gone? The last breeding group of coypus was found on the River Great Ouse near St Neots in April 1987. Two more were killed on the roads in 1988, one at Barton Bendish, one at Peterborough, but these were old males and unlikely to be members of an active breeding group.

By 10 January 1989, twenty-one months had passed without a single sighting. The time of the East Anglian coypu had passed, to the delight of marshmen, boatmen, basketmakers and graziers everywhere. A great sigh of relief could almost be heard to rise above the marshes. Yet for all their destructive powers, coypus had their own appeal and have passed into East Anglian folklore. For a time there was even a cartoon called 'Coypu Capers' in a local magazine. But maybe the last laugh will be on the coypu. Watch out for the revenge of the large furry rodent with the big front teeth and an extraordinary taste in sedge and willow.

Stone Curlew and the last Reeve

The wild wailing cry of the stone curlew, or Norfolk plover, is still to be heard across the wastes of Breckland. In the '30s this summer visitor was still breeding abundantly throughout Breckland as well as on Massingham Heath, Roydon Common, West Acre, between Fakenham and Kelling, between Burnham Market and Brancaster and on Kelling Heath. The bird also bred on heathland north-west of Norwich – Honningham, Taverham, Drayton and Swannington.

There had been fears that as the greater part of Breckland was afforested by the Forestry Commission, the stone curlews would be forced to leave. But in fact the birds have shown remarkable adaptability and now nest in forest rides and clearings throughout the area.

But numbers aren't what they were. As myxomatosis solved one local ecological problem, a rabbit surplus, it also caused another. Fewer rabbits meant more vegetation, so that the natural habitat of the stone curlew, stony bare ground, began to disappear under an onslaught of grass and herbs. This may have been good news for rabbit-stricken farmers, but it didn't suit the stone curlew. In the event, only areas grazed with sheep or devoted to intensive military activity remained suitable.

Nesting curlews are disrupted by intensive farming practices. They often nest again in the same season, so the birds are to be found in the area relatively late in the year, right up until October in some cases. The Brecklands are their natural home and they are uncommon in Broadland and the Fens. There are a few scattered breeding sites in North Norfolk, near Holt, and there are also some in the north-west between Thornham and Great Ringstead and near South Creake.

The stone curlew remains a rare bird by any standard, but it has shown remarkable adaptability. You may have trouble spotting it amongst the stones in an average Brecklands stony field, but you may be lucky enough to hear its distinctive call. At twilight, a series of blurred whistles increasing in pitch and volume ending with a climactic 'Kur-LEE' give away the presence of this shy retiring bird.

One other bird of East Anglia which has fared less well in the natural history of the area is the ruff, a beautiful bird known for the elaborate crest of white or chestnut encircling the neck of the male. The Elizabethans took the name of the bird for their own ruffs, the collars immortalized by Queen Elizabeth I and now worn by many a church choirboy.

The decline of the ruff breeding population has been attributed to drainage and reclamation of the Fens, but trapping has also played a major part. By the end of the nineteenth century, man's greed had robbed Broadland of its nesting colonies of ruffs. In older times the birds were caught by means of a horse-hair snare, but just as frequently the adult birds were shot and robbed of their eggs. As the bird became more rare, so the collector's desire increased. By 1870 the breeding stock in Norfolk was extinct, apart from one or two pairs still attempting to breed at Hickling. They stayed a gallant course until 1890. After that the only attempts were in 1907 at Hickling and 1922 at Cley.

The redoubtable Miss Emma Louisa Turner deplores the

destruction of the ruff as a native breeding bird in her book *Broadland Birds*. She recalls a 'never-to-be-forgotten day' in May 1909 when there was a huge influx of about 200 ruffs and reeves. She got a closer look at some of the birds: 'They were in splendid plumage; two of them wore ruffs of the conspicuous white variety, and one was a glowing chestnut colour.'

In 1923 she watched a party of ruffs arrive, soon to be followed by several reeves. 'As soon as the latter came, the Ruffs began to play and spar, and we had great hopes that some of them would remain to breed. But as soon as the Harriers began to work over this hill of Ruffs, they disappeared.'

Man tried to repair the damage done by his predecessors by importing birds and introducing them at Cley. Two attempts, in 1939 and 1957, both failed. Now these once-resident birds are only passing visitors. In spring large numbers pass through Hickling and Cley. In 1958, 80 to 100 were seen at Cley, and in April 1965 about eighty-five were seen at Hickling. Unlikely places like Wisbech Sewage Farm still bring them in. But they are also to be seen on grazing marshes, brackish pools, beet factory settling ponds and in autumn on tidal mudflats and also ploughland, stubble and coastal golf courses.

Kingdom of the Otter

The otter is one of those animals that everybody knows and loves but only a fortunate few have ever seen. We know the beast from favourite books – *Tarka The Otter* and *Ring of Bright Water* – but in real life he's elusive, and one is lucky indeed to catch sight of an enigmatic stream of silver bubbles in the river as he disappears. Added to this natural shyness is the fact that the otter has become extremely rare, the victim of organo-chlorine pesticides, destruction of its habitat and human persecution, with the result that it is now impossible to see an otter in most parts of England. A very small number have clung on in East Anglia against all the odds, but the chances of such a small, isolated population persisting without active help from man are slim.

Fortunately there are people who are committed to giving the otter this helping hand. In contrast to the alien coypu, for whom the powers-that-be spared no efforts to bring about its earliest extinction, the otter is a strictly protected animal and it is a serious offence to kill one or even to disturb one in its 'holt'. But even with this kind of protection the otter would probably disappear from East Anglia without more positive actions. A single death could wipe out most of the population, and the nearest populations in England and Wales are too far away to allow such losses to be replaced by wanderers from elsewhere. Because of this, the Otter Trust was established in 1972 to conduct a programme of captive breeding and reintroductions.

The Otter Trust, which has its headquarters in Earsham near Bungay in Suffolk, was founded by a couple of otter enthusiasts, Philip and Jeanne Wayre. Philip Wayre has been breeding otters in captivity since the 1960s, and his dream was to establish a surplus of young otters which could be released back into the wild. It was not, however, until 1983 that he was able to fulfil this dream and release the first one back where they belong.

Reintroducing animals back into areas where they have become scarce or extinct is a delicate business. If it is not done with sufficient care, it can condemn the released animals to a more or less rapid death. The Otter Trust has proceeded cautiously, and each reintroduction has been preceded by a careful assessment to ensure that all the conditions are right. The chosen river must have suitable habitats and a healthy fish population to feed the otters. It must not be already occupied by other otters or that other fur farm escapee, the mink. There must be little or no disturbance (from boats for example) and the agreement and cooperation of the bankside landowners must be sought. On top of all this, the young otters must be carefully prepared for freedom, which means, perhaps above all, that they should not have any inappropriate tameness towards human beings.

By carefully following rules such as these, the Otter Trust has been able to release otters annually since 1983. After the release, the progress of the young otters is monitored by various methods, including the study of tracks and 'spraints' or otter droppings and, in a few cases, by radio tracking. It is known that most of the released otters have successfully established themselves in the wild and that some have even

bred. In the near future it is believed that, as a result of the scheme, there will be otters in virtually all the suitable sites in East Anglia. After that, the Trust will start seeking suitable sites for reintroductions.

In spite of the success of the Otter Trust's work most of us are still unlikely to see a wild otter in East Anglia, but it is at any rate nice to know that they are there.

A Piper at the Gates of Dawn

One man who became the conscience of the wetlands of Anglia, a champion of Fen, Broad, marsh and mere was Ted Ellis, the celebrated local naturalist and scientist. Sadly Ted died in 1986, but the results of his research and writings are in evidence everywhere, in the policies of the Broads Authority and the local councils, and above all in the hard work and enthusiasm of the volunteers and dedicated professionals who fill the ranks of the Norfolk Wildlife Trust.

Ted Ellis was born in Guernsey in 1909 but brought up in Norfolk. From 1928 until 1956 he was Keeper of Natural History at the Castle Museum in Norwich. After that he concentrated on his writing full-time. He became known locally for his daily column for the *Eastern Daily Press* and more widely for his fortnightly contributions to the *Guardian*. From 1960 he also found a new audience, becoming a popular television and radio broadcaster.

In his writings and broadcasting his gift was one of

communication. His enthusiasm and joy at discovery were never absent. His articles could be on seemingly the most mundane subjects but would in fact elucidate scientific knowledge intelligently and clearly.

A man of Ted's ability could have done very nicely out of his talents, but money and fame meant nothing. Throughout his career he was offered several well-paid jobs but the pull of Wheatfen, his favourite piece of Broadland wilderness, was always much stronger. As his wife Phyllis said: 'Ted was never a money-spinner. What he made he used to give away with both hands, and he never realized his own worth.'

Ted Ellis's one full-length book, *The Broads*, has become the standard scholarly work on the area. He edited the 400-page book and wrote six of its fifteen chapters plus two lengthy appendices, and jointly wrote three other chapters with specialist contributors. Ted later saw it as one of the highlights of his career, but he hated the actual writing and never did another full-length book although he had many offers.

But perhaps his greatest legacy has been Wheatfen, 150 acres of wood and fen in Surlingham, near Norwich. He first discovered Wheatfen when its owner, Captain Maurice Cockle, came to the museum clutching a handful of shells gathered from his own dykes and waterways. Ted was fascinated and it wasn't long before he was invited to Wheatfen for a visit.

Ted wrote: 'It had twice the flora of the famous Wicken Fen; it was rich in bird life; it had Montagu's harriers breeding here, bitterns and – whilst the flowers were marvellous, of course – there was woodland going down into wet woodland, or carr, then the fens and a whole chain of little waterways, relict peat diggings of medieval times.'

So Ted Ellis set about mapping the flora and publishing an account of where all these plants were living, and encouraging his friends to come there. The result of his fervour is now worthy of a mention in the *Guinness Book of Records*: Wheatfen has become the best-recorded fen in Britain. The historical perspective and detailed records provide unparalleled information on a vanishing landscape. The record continues to this day, as new information and detail are added to this masterful tapestry.

The Ellis family set up home at Wheatfen in January 1946. In Ted's biography, author Eugene Stone set the scene: 'There was no electricity or gas, water came from a well, and the only light was from paraffin lamps. The house was bomb-damaged and it was half a mile from the village down a boggy track where no one would deliver coal to them. Inside the house it was so damp that a pair of boots left upstairs for a week grew mould. Outside it was so wet that the tide once lapped the side of the house. And they had a new baby!'

But as Phyllis recalled in the book: 'It was our idea of heaven.' The house became a happy, rambling, often riotous family home, where the door was always open to friends and, more often than not, comparative strangers. But there was one common factor – a dedication to the natural environment. Family parties and summer barbecues were regular occurrences, with the atmosphere charged up by Ellis's famous home brews, which had many an unsuspecting eminent naturalist struggling to keep his head.

Nature too was always given house-room at Wheatfen, whether it was the gull in the bathroom, the one-legged heron in the hall or the pink spiders, the 'cherished guests' of his study den, which earned their keep by destroying booklice.

Phyllis was, and still is, ever-practical. She made tea for visiting scholars and invariably managed to produce home-baked cakes to serve after a walk on the Fen. She still lives there, alone, but still a powerhouse of drive and energy, and now almost as much in demand for lectures, talks and public appearances as Ted was.

At Ted's funeral in July 1986, the idea to create a trust to continue his work on Wheatfen was born. Phyllis was at the forefront of efforts to raise funds to buy the land for the Trust and to publicize its work. Donations came in at speed; much dyke clearance work has already been completed; bridges have been built; walks and paths laid; and planning permission has been gained for a study centre.

But it's not all picnic sites, tidy paths and signboards. A formal nature reserve is not the Ellis style. Phyllis said: 'It's not so formal as most nature reserves, not this "keep to the path" business.' Indeed Ted's own philosophy was always to look after Wheatfen without really looking after it. He could not abide a 'gardening' approach to nature conservation. Instead, the Trust aims to maintain it sufficiently to prevent the gradual invasion of sallow, and to make it a welcoming place for anyone wanting to come and study from the professional scientist to people who just want the chance to wander and explore.

Ted Ellis was a natural naturalist, a man with an intense feeling for nature and a profound knowledge of his subject, and an artist and a scientist too. People like Ted not only make nature conservation possible; their example makes it a duty upon us all to respect and protect the world we live in. He was truly a man ahead of his time, a piper at the gates of dawn. But are we old enough and wise enough to understand and learn his tune?

The Ways of the Wetlands

The Wetlanders

The unsung heroes of any landscape are the people who work in it and with it, not on grand schemes of planning or drainage or even conservation, but in their everyday lives. They are part of the landscape; it's in their living and in their blood; it's in the way they regard the land, the way they take their living from it and the way they are. Their everyday actions mould the landscape for man and for nature, and give it definition as much as the skyline above or the earth below.

In the great wetland landscapes of East Anglia, the lives and habits of the working people figure large. The landscape we know today, the Broads and those parts of the Fens which remain undrained, owe much to the practices and trade of the basket-maker, the grazier, the amateur naturalist, the thatcher, the wherryman, the eel catcher and the wildfowler. These days, however, such people are the stuff of romance and memorabilia, of souvenir shops and heritage trails. Those that still work the land offer local 'colour' to the visitor. There are, however, some living still who work within a traditional vision, who operate within the modern world, but have lost none of the character and the colour of the work they do.

These are the people of the lost wilderness. There are fewer of them than before, and they are often known only to the wardens and the birdmen, who are in a sense their inheritors, but are one step removed from that special relationship, the being in touch with the wetland, with its growth and its wetness, with its colour and its seasonal changes. They are the osier and willow weavers who make baskets, mats and thatch from the wild plants of Broad and Fen. They are the wherry sailors who use the wind to do their bidding, or the boat builders who build for the new visitors. And they are the wildfowlers who, as times have changed and the years have advanced, have laid down their punt guns and double barrels for bird-spotting.

The ancestors of today's wetlanders were the fensmen of

Hereward, the graziers of Boudicca, the wildfowlers and farmers to the medieval kings and dukes who laid claim to the game and produce of the wetlands. But even up until recent years there were people who made their entire living from a diversity of wetland activities. One old Broads writer described the world of a marsh dweller, an old-style 'Broadsman' perfectly:

In winter after his day's reed cutting, he might be found regularly posted at nightfall, waiting for the flight of fowl, or paddling after the open water. With the first warm days of February he launched his fleet of trimmers, pike finding a ready sale at his own door to those who bought them to sell again in the Norwich market. As soon as the Pike had spawned and were out of season the eels began to occupy his attention and lapwing eggs were to be diligently sought for.

As the days grew longer and hotter, he might be found searching, in some smaller pools near his house, for the shoals of tench as they commenced spawning. Yet a little longer, and he began marsh mowing – his gun always laid ready upon his coat, in case flappers should be met with. By the middle of August teal came to a wet corner near his cottage, snipes began to arrive, and he was often called upon to exercise his vocal powers on the curlews that passed to and fro.

WILLIAM DUTT, The Broads

Shooting took the old-style marshman through the autumn and back into winter: an activity rightly deprecated these days in wetlands where the birds are no longer so plentiful. But in days gone by the population in the wetlands was not so great as to render the local fauna extinct, and the old marshmen weren't stupid. They, like all hunters, knew how, when and what to shoot to ensure that their game remained in due season and in plentiful supply for the next season. They performed a local balancing act, much as the reserve wardens do today: with local knowledge and their shooting skill they were able to maintain a diversity of species in the marsh. Whether this was by accident or design who can say? But it didn't always work, as we shall see later.

Day of the Marshman

If you are in the Broads, you must visit Toad Cottage at How Hill, on the River Ant. Here the Broads Authority have converted an old riverside cottage into a marshman's museum. You can get some idea of what life must once have been like by the bending willow and the water's edge. One room houses all the tools of the marshman's trade: tools for fishing and eel catching, tools for hunting and for cutting turf, for cutting reeds and willows, for fashioning craft and human culture from the produce of the wild. You can also see the sparse way in which the marshman and his family lived: the woven bed-spreads and the simple food.

The marshman lived in and from the wet, turning the produce of the damp, its flora and fauna, to best advantage. But there are specialized marshmen too: these are the official marsh managers. Today they are likely to be employees of the Broads Authority, restoring marshes to their pristine pre-war glory. But an older type of marsh manager survives still. He is the man who looks after the pumps; who manages the drainage of the marshes so that farming activities can be pursued within the wetlands.

Bob Rolls of Thurne Marsh is one of the few that remain: he has been working on Thurne marshes for over fifty years. In his time he has seen the heyday of windpumps, steam pumps and finally the coming of the electric pumps which once and for all put paid to the survival of Broadland's windpumps.

The Thurne windpumps were run by Bob's family for several generations. Bob said: 'My grandfather worked it when I was a boy and I can remember as a tiny boy I used to be climbing all over it. They were common in them days, they were everywhere.' His uncle ran a bigger windpump on the other bank of the river.

His grandfather gave up working the pump at the age of seventy. After a brief interval, Bob stepped into his shoes in 1938, and has been the Thurne marshman ever since. Now, at the age of seventy-four, he still farms much of the area but is also officially responsible for running the electric pump which keeps the levels drained.

As minder to the windpump, Bob had to watch for the wind, and make sure that the pump was up and running. The mill had to be oiled morning, noon and evening. If it ran all night, the marshman either stayed up, or got up every four hours to oil it through the night. During the day he would be working within sight of the pump to keep an eye on it.

The drainage pumps were owned by the internal drainage boards, made up of landowning interests in the area. The board would appoint a marshman. He was paid by the board a basic agricultural wage, only thirty-eight shillings a week in the 1940s, but was sometimes able to top this up with piece work from farmers for doing other jobs on their land.

At one time, each area, or level, had its official marshman. Their duties extended to general marsh management, to keeping the dykes clean of weeds, to cutting thistles in the summer and counting the cattle at least twice a day.

Bob Rolls also used to take on other work for local farmers – a bit of threshing, or sugar-beet carting. One job he remembers involved cutting the river banks for animal litter. 'It was a fairly long job, there was about a mile of it and you helped to cart it, and roll it all up into swathes to be carted by one of

those spectacular Broads sailing boats, a wherry, in this case the *Lord Roberts*.'

Those were the days when, in Bob's view, the river banks and sides of the Broads were tidy. 'Well, see, it all made work. Nobody does any today, it just grows up a tangled mess at the moment.' He can remember when the view across the marshes from Thurne village was clear and open because of the regular cutting of the banks, and the practice of using grazing cattle to keep down the bank vegetation.

According to Bob, autumn was a time for dyke drawing, or weeding. 'We used to do it by hand, the main dyke first then your side dykes. You don't do any dyke drawing today. They just grow up and perhaps four or five years later when they get really bad you just put in a digger and dig them out again.' Foot drains, the drains that run across the marshes into the dykes, were also cleared.

If he was getting paid piece-rate for cleaning the dykes, then it was measured by the 'score', short for a 'score rod'. A rod is seven yards so a score rod was 140 yards, and for that Bob would have been paid three shillings. 'If you done two score a day, you thought you was doing ever so well, you earned six bob, you see,' he said.

For Bob, the best vista in all the world was one of working pumps on a flat landscape. And the best place to see these in action was on Acle Bridge, looking towards Stokesby and Yarmouth. 'There was mills all over the place. Well that was the only power there was, they harnessed what they had,' he said.

Bob recalls that the marshes tended to flood more easily before the days of the electric pumps, which were first installed on the Broads in 1942. 'But when the electricity come along, that knocked the windmills out.' Wind is cheap power, but the repairs are not. The very first electric pump cost £100 to install and electricity cost then only one penny per unit.

'You can set these electric pumps like they are now and you can set them a-going and leave for six months and there's nothing go wrong,' he said.

After the initial electrification, wind and steam worked alongside for a while. A steam engine was installed in a shed in the dyke at Thurne. 'You worked the two. If the river banks were bad you'd have been forever using them even summer time, because this is a wet old level. There isn't all that many acres across, but there's such a big vast expanse of upland behind,' said Bob.

Coal was delivered for the steam engines in 20-ton lots. Bob remembers it cost twelve shillings a ton in the '20s and '30s. 'You had to stand there all day with them. You couldn't leave them. If your fire went out and the steam went, then that was the finish of it.' But by the end of the '40s, the steam pumps had all but died out.

Once the electric pumps became universal there was no call for the drainage boards to maintain the windpumps. 'A lot of them were getting into a bad sort of repair. They would cost, I should think, on average for repairs during the year, £60 or so. That was if you were lucky. But with electricity a penny a unit you could pump all the hours there was for £50 and there was nothing to go wrong. And for the electric you just used it whenever you want, it's always there,' said Bob.

As times changed, Bob Rolls changed with them. When the hand craft of pump management was finally displaced by electric motors, Bob turned to farming, his first trade. As he has farmed, he has noticed the return of the marshes, largely at the hands of the committed conservation bodies. Now he farms the land that he used to work as a marshman, while the marshes, by something of an ironic twist, have returned to what they once were.

Bob farms some of them under an Environmentally Sensitive

Far left: Secluded moorings on Sutton Broad.

Above: Globe flowers.

Left: Yellow flag iris (Iris pseudacorus) common in marshy or shallow water.

Right: A tranquil backwater near St Bene't's Abbey on the Bure.

Far right: Swans feeding in the weed-filled ditches that drain the Hundred Dyke on the River Ant.

Upon Dyke Wharf.

Evening light at Thurne.

Area scheme. This means that the Ministry of Agriculture pays landowners an incentive for the traditional management of grazing land, to discourage them from ploughing it up for cereals. The marsh-scapes within the ESA now look as they did before the great changes to farming methods that came in after the Second World War. Before then there was little hope of draining the land sufficiently to consider growing cereal crops.

Bob has, in his time, seen some momentous changes in farming, changes dominated by increased mechanization. He remembers what a terrific lot of work went into cutting the river banks. 'Years ago farmers wanted the bedding so bad for the cattle. Today they burn straw. They'd have had a fit even forty years ago if they'd seen someone burning straw.' He claims that now 'There is no hard work at all, whereas years ago you were either handling a fork all the time or a hoe or a scythe or a rake. There's none of that today, you're just sitting on a blinking seat!'

Bob's reminiscences can dispel a few myths about the decline of the wetlands through modern farm development. We tend to think of cereal crops being grown on marshland as a twentieth-century phenomenon, but Bob learned from his grandfather that in the 1880s nearly all the marshes round Thurne were ploughed up. He still has in his possession 'dibbles' used for setting or planting wheat on the marshes. They were given to him by an old man he once knew who could remember his grandfather and grandmother using the tools. 'I've heard them say that beans used to grow ever so well on there as well,' he adds.

Bob still casts a fatherly eye over the Thurne pump once in a while. He is as nimble as ever up the narrow ladders and still marvels at the engineering skill which went to build the pump. But it's a nostalgic act. His days of windpump management, the day of the marshman, have gone.

The Willow Weaver

Basket-making is one of our most ancient and unchanged crafts, dating from at least 9,000 years ago. It is a trade that produces wares which figure in our everyday lives: rustic basket-ware and garden fences, and once basket-work was used in making sails and even house-building – in roofs, doors and walls.

It is made possible by the remarkable pliability of the wetland willow. Willow sets cut from established trees are planted into ploughed and fertilized ground, and reared like any crop, except that they are only cut every two or three years, and then only the stems of quick new growth. The stools that remain form osier beds which continue to grow new shoots for cutting. The stems are cut in winter when the sap is down and the green, or wet, rods or the sun-dried brown rods are either split or left whole for weaving. They are soaked to make them pliable for working. But the cream of the willow wands are the white ones: stems which are stored in water from winter to May when the sap magically returns up the stem. The bark is stripped off and left behind is a pure white rod, essence of the white Norfolk basket.

Stanley Bird, of Burgh Castle, near Yarmouth in the Broads, has been in the basket trade since he was wearing short trousers. Born in 1915, he can look back on a proud career spanning about sixty years. 'I've known baskets all my life – since I was about four or five.' He tells how his grandfather started in the basket-making business in the 1860s; he used to pile them on his head and go down to the fish market in Yarmouth to sell them, gradually building up the business.

Stanley's father and his uncles took up the family craft. It was then inevitable that Stanley himself should follow when he left school at the age of fourteen. So did his brother, and now his son and grandson are in the business. Before the war the trade came purely from the thriving Yarmouth fishing industry. This was when the herring fleets were at the height of their prosperity, working their way down the east coast, bringing with them the Scots herring girls who gutted and prepared the fish on the quayside.

Their busy time was the autumn herring season, known as 'home fishing'. During the months of October, November and December, Yarmouth was the largest and busiest herring port in the world, packed with Scottish fishermen and their female shoreworkers who followed them. The drifter fleet, numbering about 1,000, ensured that Yarmouth's fish wharves were piled high with the distinctive baskets known as 'swills'.

These were large oblong wicker baskets with a bar handle across the middle. Each held just under 20 stone of herring.

'A government order was brought in which said that the baskets had got to be exactly the right size,' said Stanley. 'A man could make about 1,000 baskets a year, and in a good fishing season we always reckoned on needing about 10,000 baskets so we'd take on about ten men. If the fishing was poor then you'd have to stand people off – they'd go to other jobs, dockers, or on the dole.' A swill before the war cost five shillings, 25p. Today, if you bought one as a log basket it would cost over £30.

Winter months were spent repairing the baskets. After the home fishing was over there would be the osier harvest to finish. The shoots were cut from about November to April. Then the men would start to build up their stocks for the coming fishing season.

The Second World War brought major changes. The herring trade all but ceased, and Stanley went to war. He was a prisoner-of-war in Italy and Germany. When he came home and was finally demobbed in 1946 it was to find his father's works had been bombed out of all recognition. But undeterred, Stanley started anew: 'The day after I got home I started making baskets again.'

He started in little more than a shed built out of the old wood from his father's bombed factory, in Runham Vauxhall, on the outskirts of Yarmouth. By the time his brother came out of the army there was enough work to

support them both, so another section was added to the shed.

Gradually the fishing picked up again and Stanley soon found himself with an order for 3,000 baskets, but he couldn't get the materials. So while a few strings were pulled to get the willow he needed through quickly, he worked on repairing old pre-war baskets. But in time the trade again changed: as Stanley said 'I could see fish work was going to come to an end in Yarmouth.'

So Stanley diversified into supplying 90 per cent of the world's hot air balloon baskets. And there are other products: hampers for Sydney Opera House, and for theatre props.

As he says, 'A basket-maker today has got to be versatile. Before the war it was simply fish baskets. You knew from the time you left school at fourteen until you retired that you'd be making nothing but fish swills.'

The product might have changed, but the techniques have remained unaltered for 200 years. 'It's still exactly the same. There's no machinery. You've still got to sit on the floor with a plank, a box and a lapboard and make them just the same,' said Stanley. The only piece of machinery which has been introduced is a machine for stripping the willow.

Stanley's firm grow their own osiers because they cannot always get the quality they want elsewhere. But they don't grow willows. The other good source of supply in Britain for willow is Somerset: 'They can grow a good willow but not a good osier. In Norfolk we can grow a good osier but not a good willow. And they're two different things.' Osier is more liable to snap and is used for round baskets, while willow is more pliable and is used on square ones because it doesn't break when the makers bend it round the corners. In botanical terms, both are species of willow, but we wouldn't argue with a marshman.

Stanley Bird's firm owns about thirty acres of marshland at Burgh Castle where the osiers are grown. 'It's really better to buy them than grow them because it costs so much to cut them. It's got to be done by hand with a sickle and you can't get the people to do it.' It's a comment on changing times and the loss of proper wetland land use, that the farmers of the Norfolk Broads no longer grow willows as a crop. As Stanley says: 'Most of the old wetland farmers would grow an acre or two and we'd get them from all over the Norfolk Broads – Martham, Hickling, Catfield, Rollesby. We never went down to Somerset for them in those days.'

Stanley's magic wands have to be imported; a loss to the wetland landscape and economy of East Anglia no doubt, though maybe to the advantage of another area.

The Eel-catcher

Another marginal figure of the Anglian wetlands is the eel-catcher. A sighting of this solitary hunter of the misty morning Broads is a treat for any wetland watcher, and now sadly as rare as a view of a Will o' the wisp. Eel-catchers once so common, are now a dying breed.

They inhabit a solitary twilight world with a lifestyle somewhere between that of an old marshman and a country poacher, keeping themselves to themselves, as any might whose lives depend upon the wet and the quiet of the open marshes. Cecil Chipperfield of Blofield Heath is one of the few that remain, and as he testifies, the eel-catchers in general don't fraternize. He will jokingly recall how it was 'daggers drawn' when he met fellow eel-catchers, with accusations of poaching each other's patch.

Cecil, universally known as Chippie, came to eel fishing late in life at the age of seventy, with a lifetime's experience in the ways of the Norfolk countryside, including coypu trapping, already behind him. In his time he has, as he says, 'caught many a rare eel', all round Norfolk and Suffolk. But most of his catches have been made at Ranworth Broad where he was given a licence from the Norfolk Naturalists' Trust which owns the Broad. Now eighty-two, Chippie gladly imparts his reminiscences, and the odd secret of his craft along with it.

Chippie says 'I've seen them. I can remember as a little boy seeing a man with an old bramble wrapped round a huge eel – and that had happened on the land.'

He has caught some impressive eels in his time, including one weighing 8lbs and several about 5lbs. Once he even caught a pink eel. Puzzled, he took it to eminent local naturalist Ted Ellis who tried, but failed, to explain its coloration. In the end the pink one went to Norwich Museum. Chippie never heard what happened to it. Perhaps it was eaten by accident by a hungry archivist. If you happen to be in the Museum, ask about pink eels and wait to see the expression on their faces.

A prized catch for any eel-fisherman were the 'silvers', silver-bellied eels returning to the Sargasso Sea, thousands of miles away, where their life began. 'If you can catch them, which we did, they were worth a lot of money,' said Chippie.

Hardly surprisingly, Chippie has tasted and cooked a few eels in his time. 'When we were kids we more or less had to, we were so poor. My mother used to boil them up. There weren't no hanky panky, you ate them whether you liked them or not. They've got a flavour all of their own . . . I would only say they taste like eels,' he laughs.

Chippie's season would finish in September. 'They'd still catch eels right up to Christmas, but the trouble was you might go whole weeks and you might not get any. I went a fortnight once and caught three.' A good time was when the fish were spawning. 'The eels come after the fish spawn. I've had it so sometimes I couldn't lift them into the boat. I know I was busy lifting them into the boat once and I turned round and the boat was sinking, with water coming over the back,' and Chippie roars with laughter at the memory.

One of Chippie's more colourful experiences was when he had to provide a hundredweight of eels for a film crew making a film of an Arthur Ransome story. He all but despaired when the actors kept allowing the eels to escape, and in the end had to hide out of camera shot, on all fours, keeping his hands over a bucket of eels so the crew could film the sequence.

But Chippie's eel-catching has come to an end. The old catcher's nets and his feet are well and truly up. He lives by his memories, memories of life before the eel catching, memories of childhood hardship, of missing out on the Great War, of becoming a coypu hunter and a man of the marsh.

Sam the Thatch

Thatching is an ancient and well-tried craft, producing roofs that really do keep the elements out. It is that quintessentially British building style, the chocolate-box image of greener and pleasanter times. Sam Hewitt, now sixty-two, has been thatching since his teens.

As a country craft it has hardly changed since the Middle Ages and thatchers have been able to benefit very little from technical advances which have helped other trades. The tools of the trade are few and simple, the materials are provided by nature, but the two are blended together with skill to provide a roof-covering that not only looks lovely but lasts.

Traditional thatchers are solitary men; they learn the craft often from their fathers or else through a long apprenticeship. Sam started with his dad at thirteen. 'I used to do the fetching and carrying, the knocking and cleaning.' But before taking it up full-time he had a spell at sea with the herring fleet.

He started on his own by doing thatching jobs during lean times while working on the land. When he was finally made redundant from the land, he decided to make a go of thatching as a business.

'I had a little money by me and I bought transport – an old three-wheeler which was all I could buy because I hadn't passed my test.' Sam still hasn't passed his test, so still drives the three-wheeler. He has no telephone; anyone wanting to book him for a job has to come and find him at his Stokesby cottage. When they arrive he is quite likely to be walking the dog or counting cows for a friend on a nearby field. His order book is full, with almost a year's work booked up.

Thatching has become something of a trendy craft for youngsters to embark on and Sam is constantly being asked to take on apprentices. But he already has someone working for him whom he simply refers to as 'my man'. It is likely also that his son Graham will come in with his father to make the third generation Hewitt thatcher.

Like a true countryman, Sam grows and cuts his own reed for his thatch. He rents riverside land from local farmers, tends his precious crop throughout the growing season and then harvests it by hand with a scythe.

Once it has been cut he moves it by boat. In the past he has used an old wartime landing craft – since sunk – belonging to a fellow reed-cutter. It has then to be loaded on to his 'man's' motor and trailer. He has at times carted 200 bunches this way. He spreads his hands and, with thumb-tips touching, will tell you that the proper size of a bunch was three of those round.

In the past he has bought bunches half the size which cost him dearly. 'You just can't afford to buy them like that,' he says. But now, at the age of sixty-two, Sam is going mechanical. He is hoping to rent more land for more reed and is having a mowing scythe done up which he'll push through the reed-bed to do much of the hard work for him.

In his heyday Sam could cut and bunch 120 bunches a day, tie it and cart it. 'And that would be my day's work.' Now he reckons it wouldn't be possible because the reed-beds are thinner and you have to go further to gather the reed. Why is this? He shakes his head and says with some feeling: 'I don't know, but I know which is the best and that's where there's water. People say you want drains, well yes you want a few drains, if not the water will lay on there and stagnate, but if you can let the water on and off . . .'

That way, he says, you get what he calls 'a lovely steely reed. You can't break it. You get a lot of reed and you bend it and it snaps through – that's woody old reed, it's not steely.' He mows the reed beds every year 'do that won't come right.' And then adds calmly: 'And I'm gonna put a match to it.'

Burning 'cleanses' the reed-bed which has become clogged with lifeless reed and debris. After burning, the next crop will show a marked improvement. As Sam says: 'That'll come nice next year. But you can't burn it every year – it'll come right coarse and rough and you want nice fine reed.

'People think it's the best reed, this here coarse and thick old

stuff but it's not. You don't get so many stub ends because it's thick. When you get fine reed they are right thin. You get more, and they get in right close together and you get a better thatch.' The reed species he refers to, we know as *Phragmites australis*.

Norfolk thatchers have recently been on the defensive over criticism of the quality of their reed for thatching – a rumpus largely started when Shula and Mark Hebden, on *The Archers*, opted for foreign reed to re-thatch their cottage. Sam, naturally enough, says you can't beat his reed and was quite ready to cart some of his reed off to Ambridge to show the doubting Thomases.

Good reed comes dear nowadays. Sam can remember in his father's day cutting the reed-beds and sending the reed by wherry up the river to Haddiscoe where it was loaded onto trains and went to thatchers all over the country. They paid £24 for a hundred fathom – a fathom is six bunches. 'Nowadays they want 120 pence a bunch,' he comments ruefully. The extra he had to buy from Reedham this year cost £1 a bunch.

Sam must be one of the few working thatchers around to remember carting reed by wherry. He recalls loading it into the *Lord Roberts*, the *Albion* and the *Maud* and sailing with the wherries to Haddiscoe. Some was unloaded at the Stracey Arms windmill to go by lorry; the rest went from Stokesby.

In his father's day they would get help loading the wherries from locals, plying them with beer. 'If you got one of them loaded up and unloaded in a day you'd had enough then.'

For all his entrepreneurial activity Sam Hewitt Senior never made much money, preferring to live simply, always to be seen biking to jobs, his cycle loaded up with bunches of reed. Sam now recalls with affection how his dad, whom he describes as 'a proper old character', sometimes never got paid for jobs. 'Money didn't worry him,' he said.

Sam has inherited that lack of desire for money or material possessions. He can remember the hard days when there was nothing in the house to eat and for that reason, he says, finds it impossible to be the hard-nosed businessman and demand payment at all costs. While some thatchers might charge £600 for a square, 10ft by 10ft, Sam is content to settle for £400. He is content in his work and enjoys the ultimate satisfaction of being able to go round the east of Norfolk and admire it.

Ask him what time he starts in the morning and the answer won't be when the sun rises, but more likely 'when I feel like it. That don't bother me what time I start. I work until I think I've been here long enough. I'm not bothered as long as I'm happy and making a living – that'll do me.'

Would that the rest of the world followed his outlook!

Will o' the Wisps

There after supper lit by lantern light
   Warm in the cabin I could lie secure
And hear against the polished sides at night
   The lap lap lapping of the weedy Bure
A whispering and watery Norfolk sound
Telling of all the moonlit reeds around.

JOHN BETJEMAN, Norfolk

Spirit of Place

Folklore and local stories have a very diminished role and reputation in the history books of humankind. But in traditional societies the world over, folk wisdoms and belief in spirits, magic and witchcraft, have provided a useful service. They gave order to disorder, and understanding where there was ignorance and confusion. Dressing up reality with complete cosmologies of capricious gods and funny-looking beasts allowed people to explain the way reality works. Sadly, some of those explanations, and the rituals invoked, led to acts of cruelty and cowardice. The hunting down and murder of harmless old ladies as witches, the chasing to death of scape beasts like foxes and otters, are the best examples of this.

The old lore of the Fens and the Broads is no exception to this. There were witches and ritual hunts; there were hobgoblins, devils, ghosts and monsters. The old beliefs are recorded only in old guide books or collections of folktales, with no modern equivalents, showing that these bits of oral tradition, like the way of life that went with them, have well and truly passed from the world. The cruelty and superstitious practices have also passed away, but so too has their colour, the romance and the links with local places.

They have been replaced with new types of ghosts and witches that flicker on our television screens nightly, with new types of illusion – illusions of greed and gross materialism – and with new types of heroes and devils, whom it is not our business to identify.

But a volume on wild wetland would not be complete without passing reference to the old lost lore of the meres, mires and marshes. Much of it had to do of course with water and with wetness, with marshes and mists. There are no mermaids or mountain monsters, but there are hounds and ghost wherries, wild huntsmen and white ladies, animal lore and plant cures. Like the moving lights which appear in certain conditions above the night marsh, attributable to the activities of the effluvia of slow decay, but known locally as Will o' the wisps, they still have a magical resonance, a hint of another world behind the one we inhabit. Maybe the folk of yesteryear knew something we don't. As you read this, who knows what unseen creature, fair or foul, is behind you, looking over your left shoulder . . .?

Hounds in the Mist

A recurrent theme in local wetland lore is that of the demon dog, a great black marsh hound, with eyes like saucers and a jangling chain, that chills the dark wetland night with appalling howling. The dog is given various names, Old Shuck or Shock, the Black Dog of Bungay, Old Scarp or Owd Rugasan. Old Shuck is said to be as big as a calf, silent on his feet, padding along the hedgerows, following eerily in the steps of passing wayfarers and tracking them to their doom.

One Sunday, on 4 August 1577, according to local records, there was a fearful storm in the Broadland village of Bungay. At its height, the citizens of Bungay were huddled in the Church of St Mary, when they beheld a terrible apparition. A great black dog came 'running all along down the body of the church with great swiftness and incredible haste among the people, in a visible fourm and shape, passed between two persons as they were kneeling upon their knees, and occupied in prayer as it seemed, wrung the necks of them bothe at one instant clene backward, insomuch that even at that moment where they kneeled they strangely died.'

Could this be a clear lesson to all those who keep rottweilers or fail to pay their dog licence? The dastardly hound is clearly a kind of devil, a reaper figure, whose sighting, like that of the banshee in Ireland, signifies the approach of death. Hounds in folklore have traditionally been identified as emissaries of the devil, and ever since the coming of the Vikings, hounds have been associated with the kingdom of the marshes, the unknown element in the still marsh night. It's a bit hard on a poor old mutt you might think; but then, in the days when these stories were rife, so too was rabies.

One night, many moons ago, one of the authors of this book was staying in a cottage in Blakeney when his host decided to tell him about the local Old Shuck and how often the demon hound was seen in the village. A good yarn indeed, he thought, and went to bed thinking no more about it. Then suddenly, in the middle of the night, the entire household was wakened by a terrible blood-curdling howling from outside followed by a relentless scratching at the door of the cottage.

Needless to say, no one was brave enough to get up and investigate. All just shivered in their sheets, undecided whether it was a prank by either host or guest, or a real live (or dead) visit by Old Shuck.

In the cool light of the morning all became clear: a neighbour's dog had become accidently shut into the back yard of the cottage, and wanted to be let out. But the coincidence was a strange one, not least because the dog itself was a large black hound! Had we known about it at the time, the exorcism in the old legend of St Margaret might well have applied here:

> Still thou be still
> Poorest of All, stern one
> Nor shalt thou, Old Shock,
> Meet with me no more
> But fly, sorrowful thing.
> Out of mine eyesight,
> And Dive thither where thou man
> May damage no more.

A Ruin or Two

Everywhere has its favourite ruin, a broken-down building, abbey, castle or big house, where a pile of bricks and stones has a soul, the presence it has acquired from being lived in and looked at for years and years. And it is that, perhaps, which gives it the character we recognize, the romance in the rubble, and that special magic in moonlight or when the sun is hovering around the horizon, when it's hard to be really sure of what you are seeing.

The Broads and Fens are no exception. There are ruined windmills and churches, abbeys and castles, houses and homes with that special magic. The remains of Burgh Castle are probably the most dramatic. This was built during the third century AD as part of the defensive chain guarding the east coast from Saxon raiders. Called Gariennonum, it was situated behind a wharf on the south side of the great estuary at a spot where the River Waveney now enters Breydon Water.

The original fort was rectangular, with massive round towers built onto the outside of each corner. At the top of each tower was a socket which may have held a post supporting a roof, or may have housed pivots for *ballistae*, giant cross-bows which fired ten-foot arrows over several hundred yards.

Today only three walls remain. The fourth collapsed into the river at some stage, and many of the squared flints which once completely covered the face of the walls have long since been removed to build the nearby church.

The fort was clearly in heavy use during the Dark Ages. Graves of Anglo-Saxon mercenaries have been found near the site. And we know that about AD 631 King Sigbert gave the Irish monk Furzy a site for a monastery at the Castle. It was sacked by Mercian raiders around 650.

After the Norman conquest, the fort was occupied once more and a keep was built inside the walls but it has long since disappeared. What we have today are only the walls, and one

of the most impressive views in East Anglia, right across Waveney marshes and beyond.

Other ruins worth investigating when in the area include the forts at Brancaster on the North Norfolk coast, visible, though only through crop marks, and at Caister by the Sea. Here all that remains are a section of the foundations and a few buildings, including a later Anglo-Saxon hut. Both forts were part of a defensive line on the coast from Norfolk to Hampshire, linked by hilltop beacons as an early warning system against attacks by Anglo-Saxon pirates around AD 200.

Perhaps the finest ruin on the Broads, though, is St Bene't's Abbey on the River Bure. This has been a landmark in the area for over 1,000 years, and the subject of many a romantic painting, and many more photographs. What survives, however, is a mere shadow of its former glory. The Domesday Book reveals that a Benedictine monastery was already established in Horning before the Norman conquest, but the present Abbey is thought to have been founded in AD 1020 on land granted by King Canute, to a religious group already occupying the site under their leader Wolfric.

Canute was by no means niggardly with his endowment to the Abbey. He granted St Bene't's his manors of Horning, Ludham and Neatishead. Many noblemen followed suit, giving land, churches and rents. By the twelfth century it appears the abbey had a nice fat income. The register shows land and a mill at Swanton Abbot were leased out for a rent of four fat cockerels a year; land at Potter Heigham brought in an annual gift of beer for the monks. Other rents included eight measures of honey, one pound of pepper and cumin, and a pound of incense. At the end of the thirteenth century St Bene't's owned property in seventy-six Norfolk parishes.

The first abbot, Elsinus, replaced the timber church with a stone building – no mean feat, as the stone had to come from some distance away since none suitable was to be found nearby. Succeeding abbots continued the building programme.

Throughout its time St Bene't's remained a fairly small house but had great importance and prestige. The abbots were frequently in demand for national councils. Besides the monks – rarely more than about twenty-five – other people lived in the abbey, including servants and craftsmen. One of St Bene't's greatest benefactors was Sir John Fastolf of Caister Castle – the Falstaff of Shakespeare's history plays. He and his wife were buried in the chapel he built on the site.

But like old Canute himself, even monks on consecrated ground cannot thwart nature. In the thirteenth and fourteenth centuries, rising sea-levels and a series of great storms devastated the coast. The ripples were felt as far as the abbey. In 1287, the horses had to be brought from the stables by the river into the nave of the abbey church in case they were washed away. A significant change came about in 1327 when a licence was granted to enclose the site with a wall and battlements – part of this wall can still be seen. But not even this could save St Bene't's in its most dramatic hour of need.

In 1381 there occurred the Peasants' Rising, when labourers

strove to destroy the landowners' documents and so escape the tyranny of serfdom. Sacred ground was no barrier. On the night of Thursday 20 June a crowd of peasants streamed along the causeway, besieged the Abbey, and threatened the monks until they surrendered the deeds and charters. These were then burned.

But a character called Bishop Despenser was hurrying from the west, suppressing the revolt as he came, and had reached Norwich. The peasants thought he would head for St Bene't's, so on Sunday 23 June they returned to the abbey. Some historians believe they meant to kill the Bishop, and one even writes of a raging battle lasting all night, but no casualties of such a riot were recorded.

More remarkable still is the fact that St Bene't's survived the predations of King Henry VIII. In 1536 the King personally appointed the last of St Bene't's thirty-seven abbots as Bishop of Norwich, combining the bishopric with the abbacy. Henry charged the Abbot, in an Act of Parliament, to maintain at least twelve monks to continue the tradition of divine worship and service. In this way St Bene't's was the only religious house in England to escape the dissolution of the monasteries by Henry. But the last abbot, William Reppes, or Rugge, failed, and the last monk left the site in 1545.

The spirit of St Bene't's remains. It is still a holy place. On the first Sunday in August each year a service is held, and the Bishop of Norwich, as Abbot, preaches to a large gathering of locals and holidaymakers. Hymns and prayers and the sounds of worship once again rise up from the stones of this rather desolate but still consecrated place.

St Bene't's, like any good ruin anywhere, has a ghost. This dates from the time of William the Conqueror, when the monastery was put under seige by one of William's generals. But the buildings were so sound that the attacking forces could not make much headway, until one member of the fraternity, a janitor and lowly lay brother, did a dirty deal with the invaders. Succumbing to promises of elevation to high status, even to being appointed Abbot himself following the deposition of the present incumbent, this brother allowed the invaders in through the front door at the dead of the night.

The Abbey conquered, the invaders took no vengeance on the Abbot and the monks. But at daylight they assembled everyone to witness an extraordinary ceremony, the public appointment of the janitor as Abbot. They had kept their promise to the traitor. But he did not benefit for long. No sooner was the ceremony complete than his hands were tied and he was taken to the battlements. A noose was placed around his neck and he was unceremoniously hanged from the side. His reign as Abbot of St Bene't's was the shortest and most tragic in history.

The date of this incident was 25 May, and it is said that anyone unlucky enough to be sleeping on their boat at the Abbey moorings can see a ghostly enactment of this entire scene, culminating in the public hanging of the traitorous janitor.

A Witch of The Fens

We know of witchcraft and witch trials in the wetlands from the history books and from the sagas of the old Fenland storytellers. At one time these people were the local entertainers and sources of much local wisdom and knowledge. Some of the stories of these people have been collected by Mr W. H. Barrett, and published by him in the 1960s in a book called *Tales From The Fens*. One of the best tells the sad story of a local witch called Flora, who was active at the time of the adventurers, when the Fens were being drained for the first time, when change and uncertainty were in the air.

During the seventeenth century, many witches on the edges of the Fens were tried for supposed malicious acts on other persons, possessing familiars and the like. Cambridge City had part of its gaol set aside for the reception of witches; and there are records of members of the University testifying to a belief in witchcraft. Many persons accused of witchcraft escaped into the deeper parts of the Fens to avoid persecution, with the result that belief in witchcraft lasted longer there than in other parts of the country, and was active well into the nineteenth century, and even, it is said, up till today. Indeed, not so long ago, it was still the practice in many Fenland houses to encircle a home with various objects: holed stones, horseshoes, salt-glazed bricks and cushions stuffed with yarrow, to keep witches away.

One celebrated Fenland witch was known as Flora. She was the wife of a Scotsman who used to run a wayside tavern in the Fens at the time of Cromwell. The tavern was a popular spot for the Slodgers and Fen Tigers, the wildfowlers and local fenmen, to drink the evenings away, and no doubt moan about the activities of the Dutch draining engineers who were ruining their livelihood. Her husband, however, became a victim of his own brew. During the course of making one concoction, he blew himself up and destroyed the thatch of his tavern. Flora then ran the tavern herself and even played her husband's bagpipes to amuse the guests and attract newcomers.

One day, however, her playing disturbed the horse of none other than King Charles. The King was thrown into the ditch, and vented his fury on poor Flora. Her tavern was razed to the ground and Flora was whipped by the King's attendants. The spot where the King fell is known as Wag's Ducking and can be found as a ditch running near the Hundred Foot Level. Flora took to the roads and the marshes, and having lost her livelihood, clearly lost her mind as well.

She soon was blamed for every bit of bad luck that befell anyone, and there were reports that she could be seen on bright moonlit nights jumping over dykes in the shape of a big black dog. In the end the poor woman was accused of causing a great flood in the Fens by breaching a dyke with magic. She was sought out and taken in chains to a breach in a dyke bank. There she was tied to a stake and buried alive in the clay used to restore the breach.

When, some two hundred years later, the river had to be widened at that spot, no local person could be found to work on the project. The place was haunted, they said, and bad luck would come down on the head of anyone who interfered with it. In the end, only migrant labourers could be found to work on the dyke wall. To their dismay, they came across a skeleton still fastened to a great stake. The place became known as Witch's Hole, and is still avoided by local people who say that at certain times of the year Flora can still be heard, rattling her chain.

One up on the Swans

Conservation in the 1990s is big business in East Anglia, as it is around the world. Cleaning up the environment, protecting wildlife and restoring habitats have become an industry employing many people who labour to correct the disasters of the past. However, many of the mistakes of the past were not directly intentional. Few people deliberately destroyed the environment or plundered the wild of its natural riches. These things happened out of ignorance and sheer carelessness. A lack of respect for nature and ignorance of the consequences of interfering with it while pursuing growth, development and even survival.

The greening of western civilization and the compassion people now feel for wildlife are recent developments. In older traditional cultures the instinct for survival prevented outright environmental destruction. But species were lost and many cruelties to wildlife were perpetrated in the name of survival by individuals and even by whole societies. Hunting involves the death of birds and animals, but of itself is not harmful to the environment. Most hunters know the importance of maintaining the stocks of game that they rely upon, by selective killing and by culling rather than slaughtering.

However, in the wilderness of East Anglia, as elsewhere in the world, certain regrettable practices and traditions occurred which endangered the very integrity of that wilderness by causing vast species loss and reducing diversity, particularly of birds and plants. Wildfowling practices such as plover trapping, duck decoying, punt gunning, 'moultering' (knocking young unflighted birds off their perches), pochard netting, and duck driving all involved bird catching in large numbers, and would clearly not be acceptable today. But these were traditional techniques, part of the folk-culture of the time, and perhaps it is not up to us to judge, least of all those of us who are non-vegetarian. Some indication of how people looked on wildlife as a resource can be seen from these lines penned on the life of a 'Fen Fowler' in the eighteenth century:

> Born in a coy, and bred in a mill
> Taught water to grind and Ducks for to kill
> Seeing Coots clapper claw, lying flat on their backs
> Standing upright to row, and crowning of jacks
> Laying spring nets for to catch Ruff and Reeve
> Stretched out in a boat with a shade to deceive
> Taking Geese, Ducks, and Coots, with nets upon stakes
> Riding in a calm day to catch moulted Drakes.

The now forgotten English folk custom of Hunting the Wren hardly compares with that. Clearly, when all the hunting in East Anglia was going on, the birds were present in numbers we can only dream of today. So whether the hunters themselves were responsible for the decline in numbers, or whether it was due more to habitat loss, or a combination of the two, who can really say?

One game tradition no longer observed, but clearly not guilty as a cause of species decimation, was the practice of swan upping. This used to take place at the height of summer in the Broads.

There were two objectives to an 'upping': firstly, the labelling of the new swans of the year, known as 'swan-marking', a cut on the beak to signify ownership, and secondly, the catch of a swan or two for the dinner table. These objectives used to be pursued with considerable ritual and festivity, the odd drink and no doubt the odd quaint costume, by boatloads of swanherds carrying curiously-shaped crooks and sporting snowy plumes on their heads. The festivities included a lavish breakfast lorded over by the Mayor of Norwich and his leading burghers. Crowds came from near and far to witness the swan upping.

The swanherds were acting under the instructions of swan keepers, people who, by an Act of Parliament dating from 1483, had the privilege of keeping swans. The list of owners included local gentry and freemen, the monastic houses, the odd vicar, and managers of large institutions.

In order to make their mark, the swanherds first had to catch their swan, no mean feat when you consider the strength and pecking power of these great birds. From all accounts the cygnets were herded into a cul-de-sac and then all hell broke out as the swanherds attempted to catch them with their special crooks. Some of the cygnets were bound and taken on the boats to be transported to the Norwich swan-pit, there to be fattened and readied for the table. Roast swan was no doubt a rare and attractive delicacy in the old days. Swan upping still takes place but thankfully, in these more enlightened times, swan roasting is no more. We should not mourn its passing, but it is a shame that no pleasanter festival has been invented to replace it.

The Wind in the Reeds

The Winds of Change

If it is water that has traditionally had the greatest influence on the shaping of East Anglia's landscapes, then an influence which occurs not far behind is of that other great element of life: air, particularly moving air, the wind. Water and wind in this context are particularly interdependent, their interplay shaping not just nature but culture and technology too. The wind has been used by man to run windpumps which helped to tame and drain the wetlands and to power the sailing wherries which helped to create local wealth and establish trading relationships with the world outside.

It was once said that anyone who hadn't seen a wherry or a windmill hadn't seen East Anglia. But the time of the great wind machines has well and truly passed. Until quite recently it was difficult, if not impossible, to see a working version of either. Both were part of an era when men relied on harnessing the power of the wind. They are still there, but their

role in the traditional wetland landscape of the Fens and Broads is now a thing of the past, a piece of wetland technology that has been displaced by new and strange technologies. Sadly for the local economy and for the ecology of the world at large, the new technologies rely for their power not upon the power of nature but upon the consumption of raw materials, of petrols and plastics, imported from other parts of the world.

We look now upon wooden mills as symbols of a romantic past. That past may not have been quite as romantic as the paintings and postcards of the area would have us believe. But as we mourn the passing of the wooden sails as sources of natural power, we must celebrate the coming of new types of windmills to the British countryside, a new generation of wind generators helping to provide power for the future.

The Norfolk wherry may also be a thing of the past, but it has had a recent small revival in the hands of a few committed individuals. The new wherries may only be there for the tourists, but at least they are there. It is again possible to

stand in the middle of an apparently dry landscape, look out over the horizon and see a flotilla of sails, floating along a hidden river, looking as if they were ploughing through the land itself – one of the most remarkable sights in East Anglia. Many of those sails will belong to modern sailing boats but at least some will belong to wherries.

Times are changing. As we learn to make better use of the power that nature provides us with, in wind, bio-mass, in water and wave power, in energy conservation and energy recycling, then we may see a new role for the mill and the wherry among the other natural and cultural resources of England's lost wilderness. In the meantime, let us celebrate what has passed but is still there with us today.

The Wooden Sails

We have seen how people have strived for a living in the great wetlands of East Anglia virtually since the retreat of the ice. For the earliest peoples, the marshes must have provided for many of their needs: fish and fowl for food, reeds for thatching, osiers and rushes, and also herbal remedies for the marshland agues and illnesses which afflicted them. Over the centuries, however, the needs of agriculture have steadily overridden other necessities. Whilst on dry land it was forests which retreated before the farmer, in the Fenlands of East Anglia it was the wetlands which were tamed and dried out to allow him to grow his crops.

The wind played its part in this transformation, harnessed by man's ingenuity to move water in defiance of the laws of gravity. Initially, drainage was achieved simply by digging ditches and re-routing rivers, but soon the peaty soil shrank and the fields dropped below the level of the dykes and canals which were supposed to drain them. Pumps were then required to lift the water into these drains and, until the advent of steam and subsequently diesel and electricity, it was wind which provided their power.

Windpumps had their heyday in both the Fens and the Broads during the eighteenth century. The earliest ones were timber-built smock windpumps, only one of which survives today, at Herringfleet, in the Broads. The pump-man had to spread cloth across the sails manually, then turn them into the wind by means of a tail pole. The pump itself was a scoop-wheel which ladled great scoops of water from the lower level to the higher. Refinements to the basic design included the fantail, which automatically kept the sails turned into the wind, improved forms of sail which did not need to be spread manually and, in the nineteenth century, the invention of the turbine pump which replaced the scoop-wheel. With these improvements the area of marshland that could be drained increased, steadily turning the wetlands of East Anglia into the rich but monotonous food fields we know today.

These windpumps were operated by generations of marsh men. Often the running of a particular pump would remain for many years in the care of one family, as for example the Arnup

A touch of the pyramids: wherry Hathor *on the River Yare.*

family, which for three generations ran the Stracey Arms windpump, from 1831 to 1931. Gradually, however, the advent of more powerful technology, independent of the vagaries of the wind and more easily operated and maintained, made these marsh men redundant.

Today there are few remains of windpumps left in the Fens, but around seventy persist in the Broads and form a characteristic feature of the landscape, standing like sentinels over the flat fields and marshes. Sadly none of them is still operational, though a small number are fully restored, thanks to the efforts of the Norfolk Windmills Trust. The majority are derelict and a few have suffered the indignity of conversion into 'desirable' homes.

Yet, perhaps the days of harnessing the power of the wind with turning sails are still not over in Norfolk. As we become aware of the environmental hazards associated with fossil fuels, wind power once again seems an attractive source of energy. It is infinitely renewable, does not pollute nor threaten to change the world's climate and it cannot 'melt down' or leave radioactive wastes for future generations to cope with. Consequently windy places are seeing a new kind of windmill being erected, high-tech giants that would have startled Edmund Lee, the inventor of the fantail windmill. The purpose of these giants is to generate electricity, and a whole forest of them is envisaged off-shore from the Norfolk coast. Perhaps the electricity they produce will go in part to power the age-old task of pumping water to drain the levels of East Anglia.

Whither the Broad Sails?

The ancestry of the wherry goes back to Roman times. Archaeologists have suggested that a fleet of river barges must have existed to carry supplies to far-flung areas of Norfolk and to carry building stone and other materials to Caistor St Edmund, near Norwich, and Caister near Yarmouth.

One of the best known fore-runners of the wherry was the keel, a square-rigged, single-masted boat which could carry huge loads along the rivers, the main transport arteries until recent times.

But keels had a big disadvantage. Because of their primitive rigging, they could not sail close to the wind. If the wind was head-on, they either had to row or be towed, or wait until the wind veered. The change came with a revolutionary rigging from the Dutch called fore-and-aft, which meant boats could sail closer to the wind and so make progress against headwinds.

It appears that the earliest successful application of the new rig was on passenger rowing boats, mainly seen on the Thames, which were known as wherries. It is unlikely that the wherries we know now were developed from keels. A keel could not be converted to the fore-and-aft rig because it would have meant moving the entire mast structure.

So for some 200 years wherries and keels were built and worked together. The first recorded wherry, the *Spread Eagle*, appeared in the early seventeenth century, while the keels were trading as late as the end of the eighteenth century.

The New Port and the Watermen

In the early 1700s, Norwich was said to rank third of all the cities of Britain in wealth and trade, exceeded only by London and Bristol. Coal, wine, fish, oil, Irish yarn and heavy goods were imported to Norwich through the port of Yarmouth. No sea-going vessel of reasonable size could navigate the Yare so all goods had to be transferred to wherries or keels.

Exasperated by the delays in transhipment from Yarmouth, in the early nineteenth century the burghers of Norwich decided that they wanted a port for their city too. A team of city businessmen hatched a plan to make the river navigable for sea-going vessels right up to Norwich. But Yarmouth jealously guarded its position, and there was much opposition. They tried another tack, no more popular with the folk at Yarmouth, but possibly more practical than a huge drainage and bank-widening scheme up the river Yare: a revolutionary plan was produced to excavate a new harbour and channel at Lowestoft.

It involved building a lock between Oulton Broad and Lake Lothing and digging a new dyke from St Olave's to Reedham. This was completed in 1833 after much opposition. However, the new waterway between Norwich and Lowestoft was not well used. The complementary plans to build an enclosed dock at Norwich collapsed and the project was abandoned. The wherries and keels continued to ply the old routes, and the burghers of Norwich were forced to become accustomed

Overleaf: Controlling the flow into Oulton Broad at Mutford Lock (left).

A wherry party on the River Bure (right).

once again to the prospect of their goods coming slowly.

Wherries carried virtually anything which had to be moved: coal, grain, salt, sugar, tobacco, molasses, rope, oil, pitch, tar, nails, reed, city refuse, bricks, ice for the fishing trade at Yarmouth and Lowestoft, farm produce and manufactured goods from Norwich.

Some such cargoes required considerable ingenuity to transport. Hay was to be seen stacked high above hatches, while timber would frequently over-hang the sides. It is hardly surprising that a good deal of pilfering went on, some on quite a grand scale. One Henry Searle, of Bungay, was murdered by three men he had discovered robbing his wherry. The master of the *Betsy*, William Buttle, was attacked with brickbats when it was discovered that he was employed as a kind of spy to find out who was pilfering from merchants.

If any of the watermen was caught, the penalty was harsh. The master of a wherry from which malt was taken was sentenced to transportation for fourteen years. But pilfering persisted in spite of such deterrents. The Broads at that time were a lonely place and any party of police or merchants could be seen coming for miles across the marshes.

Smuggling was also rife and provided many a wherry master with a second income. Tea, gin, brandy, tobacco and silk were most in demand. It is thought that windpumps and riverside barns served as handy hiding places, and the story goes that windmill sails were used to send messages across the marshes, warning of approaching revenue men.

The contraband cargoes usually landed on dark nights on deserted beaches north of Yarmouth, particularly Horsey, to be carried across the marshes by cart and loaded on to waiting wherries. By day the wherries would conceal themselves in the reeds in some lonely spot, and carry the cargo by night.

It all made for some good yarns about encounters between the customs men and wherrymen. One such story goes that the Royall family were running an illicit cargo bound for Norwich one night when they saw the sail of a custom house cutter behind them. There followed a chase up the Yare, until the crew was caught at Thorpe. They were arrested and sentenced to twelve months in Norwich Castle jail. The court ordered the confiscation and burning of their wherry, a severe blow because, for the watermen, the wherry was their main means of earning a living. But before the customs men could get their hands on it, friends of the Royalls had acted quickly: they slipped away and sailed the wherry up to Oulton Broad.

There they sunk her, and when the prison sentence was up, the wherry miraculously reappeared again, wet and sticky no doubt but all in one piece and easily brought back to life: a clear case of *resurwrecktion*.

Life on Board

Local writer, James Wentworth Day, can find little but praise for wherrymen in his writings on the area. He tells a delightful tale of wherryman Ted Beales, of Hickling, who sailed a wherry called *The Emily*. Ted would never sail on a Sunday, being a religious man, and no matter where he was, he would moor up and trudge across the marshes to worship at the nearest chapel.

It is tempting to romanticize the life of wherrymen. To us now the Broads are a playground for relaxation, for enjoying the best that man has left of nature to offer. But wherrymen had a living to earn in all weathers, and a physically demanding lifestyle.

They frequently carried their families on board, with the wife acting as first mate, and all the tensions and passions, trials and pleasures of family life being conducted in very cramped conditions. This practice held its dangers too. In 1886 two boys drowned after falling from a wherry moored at Brundall.

In later times, the family usually acquired some small marsh cottage, and it was not unknown for a wherryman with a growing family to work his boat single-handed to save paying a mate. But this perhaps made what was already a hazardous way of life into a dangerous one. During the 150 years or so that wherries sailed, there grew a catalogue of accidents, mainly drownings.

Life on board was basic. The hub of the cabin was the stove, suitable for little more than boiling and frying. Later craft had larger stoves with the luxury of an oven. In summer the stoves made the cabin unbearably hot, so cooking was done on the deck. In Yarmouth, in the early nineteenth century, fires were forbidden on boats moored at the quay, so the cooking had to be done in sheds.

Most wherrymen were educated only in the behaviour of winds, weather and tides, and they seem to have been looked on by outsiders with suspicion. Pitifully low wages obviously led some to crime, giving rise to the perhaps undeserved jibe from other members of the wetland community that the 'only good and honest wherryman was a dead one'.

From Traders to Pleasure Boats

The wherry's time finally came up when they brought in the railways, motorized transport and new roadways. The great black-sailed traders could compete only on one count: noise. They were altogether silent, driven only by the wind. The last wherry, the *Ella*, was built in 1912 (coincidentally, the last windpump was built in the same year). But it wasn't long before the wherry's day as a viable cargo carrier was all but over. By 1949 there was not a single trading wherry under sail.

But the last of the wherrymen made a valiant effort at prolonging the working life of these noble boats by turning their hands to 'a-pleasuring'. Around the 1880s, the Broads became popular for holidays. When there was little work around, some wherrymen saw their chance and swept the hold, slung a few hammocks and offered their boats for hire for holiday cruises.

This was put on a less casual basis when enterprising owners decided to convert their trading wherries fully to pleasure wherries. Among the pioneers were Press Brothers of North Walsham. In 1888 they advertised the wherries *Bertha, Elsie, Kate, Diligent* and *Lucy* for hire. They had two cabins, one for ladies, one for gents, the latter serving as a dining saloon during the day.

The hatches were raised, the sides fitted with windows and the holds partitioned. These were all alterations which could be easily changed to allow the wherries to revert to a bit of trading (or smuggling?) during the winter. One alteration seems in retrospect a bit strange: to create space for a piano. This it seems, was, to the Victorian and Edwardian holidaymaker, what the colour TV is to today's boating tourist.

Pleasure wherries were let with a skipper to sail them and a steward to cook and wait on the holidaymakers. Some wherrymen were not averse to taking the holidaymakers for a bit of a ride. The less scrupulous found it paid dividends to get their wives to send them a telegram wishing them happy birthday. It always proved good for a whip-round or a few pints in the pub. So too, it was also not purely for the well-being of the hirers that wherrymen would insist the best mooring site was alongside a pub.

Walter Rye, in his book *Songs, Stories and Sayings of Norfolk*, published in 1897, had a few words of advice for crews on how to treat their skippers. 'All sailors, fresh and salt, have an invincible distaste for tinned meat and will do without rather than eat it. Nothing makes a yachtsman so unpopular as to try and work his wherry or yacht on tinned provisions and open mutiny is often the result.' He advises it is best to share food with the wherrymen and warns they drink plenty of beer.

The story goes, according to Mr Rye, that one hirer was flabbergasted when his crew asked leave to go ashore to visit the dentist. When asked why, they replied they were going to get all their teeth pulled because they obviously had no use for them on the cruise.

Most yachtsmen working on pleasure craft, he claimed, were hardworking and civil men. But some, he warned, 'get a bit above themselves through the unwise liberality of Londoners who come down for a week or two and don't mind living at the rate of £10,000 a year for that time, thus spoiling the men and "haining" the market for the regular boat-owners.'

In 1907 a party of eight would have paid about £14 a week to hire a wherry. The cost included provisions – 'best hamper, including fresh-cooked meat'.

Many people who hired pleasure yachts fairly lived it up. Walter Rye calculated that a party consisting of a doctor, two captains and a lieutenant of a Midland militia regiment managed to put away 186 bottles between them during one week. The drinks included 72 bottles of champagne, 24 bottles of spirits and 24 bottles of sherry. Each man must have drunk about 6½ bottles a day.

Pleasure wherries, while often beautifully fitted out inside, had little room for lounging on deck. So, ever adept, the Broads boatbuilders began to develop a new boat, the wherry yacht, with a carvel or smooth-built hull, and a counter stern which gave room for the Edwardian parties to enjoy the scenery. While the visitors all lived in luxury, however, the master and mate on these wherry yachts had to live in more cramped conditions. Their cabin was the tiny forepeak which housed the great iron counter-weight for the mast.

The Phantom Wherry

Thanks to tourism, the wherry was given life after death, but even so, only seven wherries out of the tally of hundreds remain on the Norfolk Broads. Six are afloat and one is undergoing restoration. Some of the rest can be found at Surlingham Broad, part of a wherry graveyard where the rotting hulls and sides of these great beasts of burden have been put to good use stopping banksides from erosion by modern boatwash.

Foremost of the rescued wherries is the trader *Albion*, owned by the Norfolk Wherry Trust, which is sailed on cruises throughout the season. She is unusual in that she was the only trading wherry which was not clinker built. *Albion* was carvel built to avoid snagging on the side of locks.

Another wherry, *Maud*, is undergoing painstaking restoration at the hands of Vincent and Linda Pargeter at Upton Dyke. She was rescued from the mud of Ranworth Broad where she had been deliberately sunk to shore up the bank. Before the Pargeters could remove her they had to replace her with another hulk.

There's one famous wherry that is not likely to be rescued from the deep, and this one is the subject of a famous local ghost story. According to this, one old wherryman used to ply his craft carrying wheat from Lowestoft and Yarmouth to Beccles. He always delivered it to the same mill, and part of the attraction was the miller's beautiful daughter.

The innocent young woman had no idea of the wherryman's passionate desire for her. He invited her to sail with him down to Yarmouth, and father and daughter agreed to the plan. When she went down below to make tea for them he followed her and set upon her. But the maiden was not ready to give up easily. She escaped his clutches and, grabbing a knife with which she had been cutting a cake, she leapt on deck. When he lunged towards her, she struck out with the knife, wounding him beneath the ribs. He fell overboard, the legend goes, with a hollow, soul-searching scream.

The maiden collapsed, exhausted, and it was not until

nightfall that she looked around her and discovered with horror that the wherry had drifted out to sea. Watchers on the shore had seen the sail get smaller and smaller till it disappeared over the horizon. Then they saw a tongue of flame leap towards the sky, hover for a moment, then slowly go out.

Nothing was seen of maid nor wherry ever again. But on the anniversary of this tragic event, a phantom vessel is said to sail down the winding reaches of the Waveney. The hull is no longer black, but a shimmery white, and the sail above floats like a dazzling, terrifying expanse of rippling flame. The intensity and brilliance of the scene scorches the eyes of the watchers till they can bear to look no longer. When they look again, everything is black, and a strange smell of burning is said to linger in the air.

Who Pays the Wherryman?

Peter Bower is the nearest you can get to a wherryman in the Broads today. In partnership with Barney Matthews, he runs Wherry Yacht Charter, a fleet of two wherry yachts and one pleasure wherry, carrying on the tradition of wherry holidays started in Victorian times.

He slips easily into the role of wherryman. For several years, before he devoted himself full-time to the charter business, he worked part-time as a teacher at Cromer High School. In true wherrying tradition he would set off on a cruise carrying his bicycle in a dinghy behind the wherry. When the day came round for him to go to school, he would row to the nearest staithe, ride the bike to the nearest station, and be in the classroom in time for the school bell.

Peter is a quietly-spoken Norfolkman who finds every attraction in the solitary, individual way of life of the wherrymen. During his fifteen years of skippering the *Olive*, Peter has acquired a growing admiration for the old wherrymen, in particular for their strength. In the early days there were no engines which could be kicked in when the wind dropped. Instead a 24-ft quant pole had to be used, often leaving whoever had the misfortune to use it with a raw, sore shoulder. 'They would have been tough. They had to load and unload the cargoes and they had to be strong doing that,' said Peter. The wherrying life makes you that way. It's solitary, and if the elements are a bit rough, you have to get a bit rough in order to win.

'There must have been good 'uns and bad 'uns, straight ones and crooked ones. They were human beings. I suppose there might have been a slight sort of suspicion of them in the same way there is with gypsies, though not to the same extent,' said Peter.

Peter's painstaking restoration of the *Olive* is a testament to his love for the boats. *Olive* was decaying fast at Tunstall, but still cost him £4,000 to buy outright. 'I went into it totally blind which I don't regret because if I'd had a survey and sat down and thought about it I'd have realized I couldn't afford it,' he said.

Her condition was 'grotty', the mast, gaff and sail all needed replacing, as did some of the planking. He consulted a retired boatbuilder, who had worked on wherries, and learnt by trial and error. 'I soon realized the only way I could manage it was if I did a lot of the work myself,' he said. But he got it right and was able to start chartering in 1977. His first customer was the Lord Lieutenant of Norfolk, an auspicious start, for his family, the Colmans, had an association with wherries. It was two Colman sisters who had commissioned the building of the pleasure wherry *Hathor*, a boat famous in the Broads for its origins.

Return of the Hathor

Peter Bower and Barney Matthews bought the *Hathor* in 1985 from a boatyard at Martham where it had been retired as a houseboat, and they restored it for pleasure trips up the Broads. This extraordinary boat has presented them with new challenges and taken them back to the early days of wherrying when engines were unheard of. Still the only remaining pleasure wherry which can be chartered on the Norfolk Broads, she is an elegant craft with a fascinating history.

Hathor, pronounced 'Heart-or', was built for Ethel and Helen Colman, daughters of Jeremiah James Colman who established the famous Norwich mustard firm J. & J. Colman. They had a younger brother, Alan, who at the age of twenty-nine began to show signs of tuberculosis.

The family moved him from their home in Norwich to the sea air of Corton, near Lowestoft, but to no avail. He suffered a relapse and they decided the dry, clean air of North Africa would prolong his life. In November 1896 he set sail with his sisters Helen and Laura, bound for Egypt.

Alan got worse, but he was fed up with being stuck in a hotel even if it was at the base of the Great Pyramid. He expressed a strong wish to see something of the Nile, so was taken on board the *Hathor*, one of the sailing boats common in Egypt, and began to journey up-river. It was to be his last river journey. He died a few weeks later, aged thirty.

His death upset the family deeply, and seven years later, when Ethel and Helen were commissioning a pleasure wherry, they chose to commemorate their beloved brother's last days by calling it *Hathor*, after the Egyptian goddess of love, joy, the sky and also of the west – the kingdom of the dead. They wanted the interior to be designed round the hieroglyphics of Egypt and its mythology. This was done by Edward T. Boardman, who had designed How Hill and other well-known Norwich buildings with the help of his partner Graham Cotman.

The wherry was built by Halls of Reedham at a cost of £575, excluding the internal partitions and fitting out. The Egyptian symbols used in the internal decor included the sphinx, scarab beetles, sailing boats, snakes, frogs and crocodiles. Hieroglyphics meaning joy, increase in power, life, good luck, buckle or tie, stability and verdure were also included. It turned out that the cost of the interior design was greater than the cost of building the boat itself.

Broad Horizons

Safe at last, but in whose hands?

Our story should now be a familiar one, of wetlands lost and found, of a wonderful slice of natural heritage of national and international importance, which has been diminished by time and the actions of man, but the true value of which is only now coming to be appreciated. Now that we know how valuable our last wetlands are, is their future any more secure? What does the future hold for the Anglian wetlands, and indeed our other remaining wetland areas?

Are they to be swallowed up by tidal waves of development? Will they be destroyed by those silent global despoilers of nature – pollution and habitat destruction? Or will they become some kind of specimen caught in a time warp, where people can come and look through telescopes at the last bittern, the last Bewick's swan, or the last marsh harrier?

Today the future of the wetlands lies firmly in the hands of the public. It depends upon the demands we make on it – for recreation, for agriculture, for development, even for transport, and last, but certainly not least, for nature conservation. We all have a part to play in protecting the Fens and Broads and their habitats, creatures and landscapes. We all have a right to enjoy their beauty, to benefit from their produce, to sail, swim, walk, drive and explore along the accepted routes.

But that right, that enjoyment, has to be managed, no longer just by the landowners but by those vested with the duty to conserve and protect: the conservation agencies, the tourist authorities, the drainage and water boards, the planners and land users. These are the strategic guardians of the wetland heritage which remains.

And to that list must be added voluntary bodies, some of them landowners and users themselves; bodies like the National Trust, the Wildfowl Trust, the Norfolk Wildlife Trust, the RSPB and CPRE, whose dedication to the cause of protection is enhanced by enthusiasm and personal sacrifice.

Perhaps the most critical agency of all is the Broads Authority, a single body charged with the task of protecting the Broads system of rivers and lakes, the most important collection of wetland habitats in the United Kingdom.

Then there are the day-to-day guardians, the wetland managers, modern-day nature protectors, a new breed of professionals and volunteers. They are the wardens, like Francis Russell at Hickling, Bernard Bishop at Cley, and Tim Bennett at Wicken Fen. They are the watchers on the landscape; benign gamekeepers with binoculars instead of guns. Their business is conservation management; their knowledge and skill has been learnt from textbooks, university lecturers, hands-on experience, and from listening to an older generation who once worked in a closer harmony with the land, because they had to.

In the fenlands around Wicken, the people once pursued a fen-friendly pattern of life, cutting the sedge, grazing cattle, cutting litter and digging peat. These were all activities which enabled the birds, beasts and mini-beasts to thrive. Now their single heir, Tim Bennett, the warden, plans his cutting regime to recreate artificially the cycle of life that ensures plants like ragged robin do not become as dead as the proverbial dodo. Where, 100 years ago, the work was done by scores of people cutting by hand, now machines do the heavy work, augmented by teams of willing volunteers who come out for the love of protecting what they believe is precious.

So too, the R S P B, the N W T and the Welney Wildfowl

Refuge manipulate water levels on their reserves to guarantee ideal conditions for birds needing a damp or watery refuge in winter. Some critics might say they are creating and maintaining something artificial and turning it into a showpiece. The answer must be that the birds wouldn't come in their thousands if they didn't like it.

The Heroes of Halvergate

These are the day-to-day achievements. They are preceded by the more historic ones: the foundation of Welney, the establishment of Cley and Hickling as reserves and the protection of Wicken. More recently, another historic conservation achievement was added to the list: Halvergate Marshes.

The Halvergate saga started when Aitken Clark, the chief executive of the original Broads Authority, discovered that big drainage schemes within the Broads did not have to come to the Broads Authority for consultation. This was despite the fact that they had the potential to change the landscape forever, in very major ways. Aitken quickly saw to it, by going direct to Whitehall, that the system was changed. The Broads Authority then had to be consulted before new drainage schemes were put in place.

One of the first drainage schemes to come before the Authority was a major and costly scheme on Halvergate, the planning for which was already well advanced. The Broads Authority turned it down. A fierce battle then raged between conservationists and the agriculture and drainage interests. The battle made national news, and the press coverage forced the hand of government. In the end, a pilot scheme called the Broads Grazing Marshes Scheme was thrashed out, which offered farmers incentive payments for managing the marshes in a traditional way. The Broads area, including Halvergate Marshes, was given a new designation, as an Environmentally Sensitive Area, the first of its type in Britain.

Aitken Clark believes that the Halvergate saga was a turning point for the conservation movement. For the first time the government was paying farmers for conservation-led farming. For the first time, traditional farming practices were given a positive status, over more intensive methods which tend to destroy the natural environment. Gone also was the notion that farmers who did not plough up the marshes for yet more arable crops were somehow losing out and were therefore entitled to high compensation payments.

The grazing marshes scheme has been a massive success, with a solid take-up from farmers. The conservationists had not only won a local battle, they had proved a critical historic point, that wetland conservation was more deserving of public financial support than the unceasing development of wild land for the production of surplus food.

A Park for the People

Aitken Clark, the hero of Halvergate, is a man who cares passionately about the Broads. He came as chief executive in 1979, giving up a high-powered job at the University of South Carolina in America, to help conserve a diminishing empire of Anglian wetlands, some 280 square kilometres in extent.

Aitken arrived at a time when the Broads Authority, formed over a year earlier, needed a sure touch at the tiller. The Authority had been set up as an experimental body in answer to a local and national cry to 'do something about the Broads'. He knitted together a team of officers and set up a series of productive working parties. These brought together diverse views and came up with practical answers to the big Broadland questions. The first, most manifest, achievement was the dredging of Cockshoot Broad, a restoration project which showed that in some cases it was indeed possible to turn the clock back. The Broad was badly silted up and devoid of its once abundant waterfowl. Now newly drained, it is home to a range of water plants, some rare, others common, that together form that complex interactive net, the wetland ecosystem. The insects and birds have returned too. The experiment set the pattern for the dredging of Belaugh and the latest project, Hoveton Little Broad.

The temporary Authority had more than proved its worth and it was recognized that a permanent arrangement was needed, a new National Park. But because of the unique nature of Broadland and its inherent differences from the other ten national parks, new legislation was needed if an authority was to fulfil its function. A private bill was drawn up and promoted by Norfolk County Council.

But the private bill went down. The bugbear was navigation. Historically the Great Yarmouth Port and Haven Commissioners held navigation powers, and they were tenacious in their bid to retain them. It was a futile gesture: it would have been illogical for the body responsible for managing a nationally important wetland not to have power over land and water space.

In the event, the government was persuaded to take the bill up. It was enacted in 1988, and the new National Park was given Royal Assent. Once again, the Broads had paved the way for others to follow. Proponents of the bill had used the basic legislative framework common to other national parks, coupled with specific additions designed to meet the need of a unique wetland area.

Still though the cry is up: 'Do something about the Broads.' With more money and more power, Britain's new and very special National Park is expected to get instant results. Aitken Clark's answer is: 'Patience. I want people to temper their expectations with the knowledge that the restoration of Broadland is a fifty-year marathon.' The programme now being implemented is long term – twenty to thirty years. But at the end of it, Aitken Clark is convinced, the result will be areas of the Broads as they once were, with sparkling water, aquatic plants, and he adds: 'the whole area will be seen as a very

special and fragile area of nature conservation which has a limited environmental capacity for tourism which must not be exceeded.'

In the past that capacity has been exceeded and the Broads have been ill-treated, particularly by pollution, mainly from nitrates and phosphates. The former comes from agriculture and is hard to tackle effectively. The latter comes mainly from treated sewage poured into the river system. Phosphates are harmful for the Broads because they act as over-zealous fertilizers. They make the tiny microscopic algae bloom to such an extent that they cloud the water, stopping life-giving sunshine from reaching the aquatic plants. The huge number of algae also change the balance of oxygen in the water, creating 'sags' at night, when the respiration of countless million microscopic plants outweighs the accumulated oxygen bank of the day's photosynthesis. The process is known as eutrophication. The plants then cannot survive, nor can the insects which live on and off them, and so the whole delicate balance is upset.

The easiest way to tackle this is to stop the phosphate being poured into the water by installing stripping plants which can remove up to 90 per cent of the phosphates. This has been done since 1978, firstly on the River Ant, and later on the upper Bure. But phosphates have built up in the mud at the bottom of the Broads over a long period, so simply turning off the tap is not enough. This is where dredging comes in. Drag out the mud from the bottom and you pump the source of the

problem away – provided you can afford the expense of a major engineering project and you can find somewhere suitable to dump the foul-smelling mud where it won't end up back in the river.

On some Broads, however, mud-pumping is not feasible, so experts have had to investigate the possibility of a little bio-manipulation. Water fleas are a crucial link in the water quality chain, as they feed on the algae. If there are enough hungry water fleas in a Broad, the pollution will literally be gobbled up for dinner. These tiny fleas have monumental appetites, but they are themselves a tasty meal for fish, so unless the fleas have enough aquatic plants to hide in, they won't last long enough to do their job. The answer is to remove the fish or to establish artificial plant refuges for the fleas.

All such experimental work has to be carried out in one of the most popular tourist haunts in the country. It requires little skill or tuition to handle a hired cruiser on the Broads. There are no lock gates to tackle; the water is fairly shallow and that chance to 'get away from it all' is readily accessible to all. The number of hire craft peaked on the Broads in the mid-'70s when well over 2,000 cruisers were available for hire. Over the next decade the figure decreased, but in 1987 it was estimated that about 200,000 holidaymakers a year still took a holiday on a hired motor cruiser.

In their wake comes the damaging wash of the cruisers. Bank erosion means an increased threat of flooding. In the past, to protect the banks, the Authority has had little choice

but to accept ugly piling, a method which makes the rivers look like canals. Not only are these unattractive, but they provide no homes for otters, bank voles, wildfowl and the other birds that traditionally nest in the reed fronds.

In their natural state, river banks have in-built protection in the form of roots, stems, reeds and submerged water plants which soak up the wash, but once the bank has been attacked it is almost impossible to regenerate growth of the plants without some sort of help. The most promising experiment has been the laying of a sort of asphalt carpet on a gently sloping bank, which gives the young water plants something to hold on to while they are getting established.

The other vital weapon in the Authority's armoury is a reduction in speed limits. Research has proved that cutting back the top speed of boats has a significant effect on erosion. Getting visitors to stick to the limits may be another matter altogether.

The holiday industry, however, in all its guises, whether it be the families who inhabit the waterside chalets or the youngsters who take the boat wheel wearing their pirate hats, is the bread and butter of the local economy. Some people may harp back to the days when the upper and middle classes came for genteel holidays in Broadland on graceful wherries and other pollution-conscious sailing craft. But those days are gone, and it is fitting that the Broads should be more than a playground for the wealthy boating fraternity, that they should be somewhere that everyone can visit, by boat, by car or on foot, to appreciate their spell-binding beauty.

The Final Balancing Act

As keepers of the remaining heartland of England's lost wetland wilderness area, the Broads National Park Authority has a delicate balancing act to perform. It has to cater to the needs of the water users, the landowners and the farmers and the needs of nature, wild and tamed. Its message for the 1990s is the promotion of 'green' tourism; an attempt to get the message across that the Broads are a fragile wetland that deserves the respect of a caring visitor, whose reward will be a glimpse of a wilderness area which is phenomenally rich in wildlife. The presence of those visitors, helping to pay the way for the present and future management of the Broads, together with careful management of all other resources, water and land based, are all part of this vital balancing act.

It is to our national shame that there is no Fens Authority, no official Friends of the Fens, able and equipped to do the same for the Fens as has been done and is being done for the Broads. But, as the statistics show, there are not a lot of Fens left, and what is left is well protected by a range of voluntary and official bodies. The Fens somehow do not attract the kind of support and emotional appeal that the Broads enjoyed. Nor do the Fens have the same public appeal for recreation, though arguably the waterways are there: the Cam and the Ouse and their tributaries.

However, the Fens of East Anglia may yet have their day. And there is, of course, another way of helping to secure a promising future for fen wetland: by creating fenlands anew. But that is another story. And maybe Mother Nature or man-induced atmospheric changes will intervene in the equation before we ever get round properly to restoring the lost wetlands of England's lost wetland wilderness.

Index